Multimedia for Learning

Development, Application, Evaluation

Multimedia
for
Learning

Development, Application, Evaluation

Diane M. Gayeski
Editor

Educational Technology Publications
Englewood Cliffs, New Jersey 07632

Library of Congress Cataloging-in-Publication Data

Multimedia for learning : development, application, evaluation / Diane
M. Gayeski, editor.
     p.   cm.
  Includes bibliographical references and index.
  ISBN 0–87778–250–4
  1. Educational technology.   2. Media programs (Education)
3. Computer-assisted instruction.   I. Gayeski, Diane M. (Diane
Mary), 1953-   .
LB1028.3.M85   1993   92–2◄
371.3'3—dc20   C

Printed in the United States of America.

Library of Congress Catalog Card Number:
92–24208.

International Standard Book Number:
0–87778–250–4.

First Printing: January, 1993.

Preface

Gabriel D. Ofiesh

Modern man is becoming more primitive. He understands
as little about the technology that serves him as primitive
people understood about lightning and air.

Jose Ortega y Gasset, *Revolt of the Masses*

Multimedia, the new buzzword, has confounded the problem.
The problem is that ignorance can lead to misuse. It has been
my experience as an observer of the use of a variety of
instructional and learning technologies (and, believe me, they
are different) over the last thirty to forty years that we use
newfangled tools to do things in old, familiar ways. We fail to
see the added inherent capabilities in the tools.

Instead of envisioning the empowerment capabilities of the
new multimedia tools and utilizing them fully, we are prone to
limit their use by our previous experiences. In other words, we
end up automating the past, as we continue beating the rug
with a fancy, new electric vacuum cleaner. It may get the job
done, but there are certainly easier ways to go about it. New
perspectives, however, are embedded in the papers that Diane

Gayeski has gathered and organized in this volume, and they deserve careful reading.

It is not an easy task to make the paradigm shift and find new ways of thinking about how the multimedia technologies can facilitate learning and empower the learner to become a more creative participant in the educational process. The multimedia technologies enable us, as never before, to help learners, at all ages, to shift from a teaching mode to a full learning culture—where the learner is in control not only of what he or she will learn but also HOW he or she will learn it.

Today, as a careful reading of the articles in this definitive text will make apparent, learning can become "interactive" in a high-fidelity sense that we never thought possible before. It will be unfortunate if we do not heed the "guidance" embedded in these articles and instead end up doing only what we have done in the past—simply piling the new technology on top of the existing classroom procedures and expecting, because we are "using multimedia," that we will solve our problems and make education the "exciting" experience that it can be.

If we limit our understanding by assuming that the computer is just an electronic page turner or that a CD-ROM containing sound, animation, and graphics is just a very large storage medium in a very tiny space, we will not be able to use the new tools to our advantage. We will have made our job of facilitating learning (no longer "teaching") even more difficult.

The authors here see and articulate the potential. For the reader to apply the various visions contained herein will require one to forget much of the past and think anew about what he or she has learned from these chapters.

For centuries mankind exchanged information only through word-of-mouth. Later, books became the primary source. As a result of the invention of radio and then television, our information sources shifted once again. With new technology, we had to give up deeply entrenched habits and learn some new ones. Now with the emergence of the silicon chip and laser (or "light" technologies, as I like to refer to them) we are beginning to rely on electronic tools which allow us to present written words, sound, pictures, and other graphic images. But, more importantly, the new multimedia tools allow us to sort, rearrange, and merge information in ways never before possible. We now have the ability to weave together heretofore disparate facts into a seamless carpet of knowledge.

Einstein said, "Ideas should be stated as simply as possible, and no simpler." The authors are to be commended for demystifying the jargon and stating matters as simply as possible, and no simpler. Profundity without pontification. To write about multimedia formats is a challenging task—which has been well-met in this volume.

There is an awareness here that the PC-based emerging technologies to support tomorrow's high-performance work systems will be designed by socially-oriented technologists. They will design—together with users—technological systems that will be in the *service of people* and their practices. The hope is that the reader-educator, after having read and mastered this text, will start to become part of this new team.

Tomorrow's approaches will be grounded in the notion that the whole is greater than the sum of the parts. Excessive compartmentalization of work inhibits collaboration. What drives collaboration and improvisation is a sense of shared vision. And who better to develop this vision than those who are committed to educating themselves and others?

In a high-performance educational system, everything—people, technology, organizational structure, teaming and work practices, and belief systems—will work together to make the organizational whole greater than the sum of its parts.

Lester Thurow, noted economist and futurist, has said, "The new technologies give us the opportunity, if we are up to it, to shape the art of education in the future." This book is a beginning.

Gabriel D. Ofiesh is Emeritus Professor of Educational Technology, Howard University, Washington DC, and currently Senior Scientist with the Institute for Technological Solutions.

About the Authors

Diane M. Gayeski, Ph.D. is associate professor and chair of the graduate program in corporate communications at Ithaca College, and partner in OmniCom Associates, a communication analysis, design, and production firm. She holds a Ph.D. in educational technology from the University of Maryland, and has been involved in pioneering work in teaching about and producing interactive media technologies since 1979. The author of *The Renaissance Communicator in Information-age Organizations* (Focal Press, in press), *Corporate and Instructional Video* (Prentice-Hall, 1983; 1991), *Interactive Toolkit* (OmniCom Associates, 1987), *Interactive Media* (with David V. Williams, Prentice-Hall, 1985), and *Using Video: Interactive and Linear Designs* (with Joseph Arwady, Educational Technology Publications, 1989) and numerous book chapters and articles, she has been invited to present over 100 workshops and executive briefings throughout the U.S., Canada, Europe, and Japan. Her work in information technologies has won awards from the Association for Educational Communications and Technology and the National Society for Performance and Instruction. Through OmniCom Associates, Diane engages in consultation and multimedia project management for clients worldwide, including AT&T, Xerox, Centro de Tecnologia

Educativa (Mexico), Rabo Bank (Holland), University of Helsinki (Finland), Bank of Montreal, Eastman Kodak, and Intel. Her current R&D projects include software tools to support instructional development, the alignment of new communication and training technologies with emerging corporate cultures and management theories, and management systems for organizational communication.

Christopher J. Dede, Ph.D. is a full professor at George Mason University, with a joint appointment in education and in information systems. He is also director of the university's Center for Interactive Educational Technology and on the core faculty for the Institute of Public Policy. Chris has been a visiting scientist at the Computer Science Lab at MIT and at NASA's Johnson Space Center, as well as a Policy Fellow at the National Institute for Education. His work centers on technology forecasting and assessment, applications of artificial intelligence to education, and strategic planning for organizational development.

Sandra Kay Helsel, Ph.D. is principal of Infinite Media, a multimedia computer and communications consulting firm. She is editor-in-chief of the *Multimedia Review* journal and the *Virtual Reality Report* and also organizes Meckler Publishing's annual "Virtual Reality Conferences" on the West Coast. Dr. Helsel's doctorate is from the University of Arizona; her dissertation research utilized curriculum theory to create a theoretical matrix for the design of educational interactive multimedia. She previously directed a multimillion dollar Eskimo-language curriculum project for the state of Alaska which produced books, teacher manuals, and training tapes in both English and the Eskimo language.

Jim Hoekema is president of Hoekema Interactive, a multi-media design and user-interface consulting firm. Starting in 1977, Jim has produced programs and written style standards for industry (IBM, AT&T), education (WICAT, Mediashare, Museum of Modern Art), and entertainment (American Interactive Media). Current projects include a multiple-language CD-I travel series for Philips/Italy, and a series of school products for the National Geographic Society. Mr. Hoekema holds M.A. and M.Phil. degrees in art history from Columbia University.

David Hon is president of IXION, a multimedia design and development firm specializing in simulation systems. He is the developer of award-winning interactive systems including the CPR Simulator, the Oxyacetylene Welding Simulator, and two endoscopy simulators for educating physicians in minimally invasive surgery. He is a frequent speaker on interactive design and has testified before Congress on the potentials of simulation systems for education and training.

Pam Knight is the multimedia production manager for the Texas Learning Technology Group. TLTG's major products include the award-winning Physical Science course, and the Chemistry course, submitted for adoption as textbook alter-natives. Pam attained a B.S. degree in Systems Science from the University of West Florida, and an M.A. degree in Communica-tions Management and Instructional Technology from the Annenberg School of Communications at the University of Southern California. Prior to TLTG, she worked as a course developer and trainer at Intel Corporation and as an indepen-dent communication consultant.

William D. Milheim, Ph.D. is currently employed as an assistant professor and coordinator of the graduate program in instructional systems at Penn State Great Valley in Malvern, PA. He has a Masters degree in health education and a Ph.D. in curriculum and instruction, both from Kent State University. His current research interests include instructional design, multimedia, distance education, and computer-based learning. He has published a number of articles on these topics in national journals and has made numerous presentations at both regional and national conferences.

Leon A. Murphy is president of Qi3, Quantum Improvement International, Inc., a total quality management and performance support company, based in the Lehigh Valley, PA. Previously, he was manager of the Bethlehem Steel Corporation multimedia applications team. He is a graduate of the University of Massachusetts at Amherst and has an MBA from Boston University. He has been actively involved in the development and implementation of interactive training and presentation systems since 1984.

Thomas C. Reeves, Ph.D., an associate professor of instructional technology at the University of Georgia, teaches program evaluation, instructional design, and research methods courses. He has developed and evaluated interactive technologies for fifteen years, and has been an invited speaker in many countries, including Australia, Bulgaria, Finland, Peru, Russia, Switzerland, and Taiwan. He is past president of the Association for the Development of Computer-based Instructional Systems (ADCIS) and a former Fulbright Lecturer. His research interests include applications of "computer modeling," electronic performance support systems, adult literacy, user interface issues, and instructional technology in developing countries.

William B. Whitten II, Ph.D. received his doctorate in experimental psychology from the University of Michigan in 1974, and served on the psychology faculties of the University of Michigan and the State University of New York at Albany. He next served as the assistant director of the Personnel and Training Research Programs at the Office of Naval Research. He joined AT&T Bell Laboratories in 1983. Since then, he has worked with a wide variety of technologies, emphasizing the increasing importance of multimedia capabilities for user interfaces, training, and performance support.

Table of Contents

good for
evaluator

Good
for
assessing
potential
of m.m.

Nwi = not worth it

Multimedia for Learning

Development, Application, Evaluation

Chapter 1

Making Sense of Multimedia: Introduction to This Volume

Diane M. Gayeski

Ithaca College/OmniCom Associates

I've been working with multimedia since 1979; back in those days it was called "interactive video" or "computer-assisted instruction." It was difficult to get a handle (physically *and* conceptually!) on the myriad of boxes and wires and software that were being developed by visionaries in their R&D labs and garages. Those were exciting times—days when we congratulated ourselves if we could successfully make a VCR and computer talk to each other and get through a program without crashing. Several years and many projects later, David Williams and I wrote *Interactive Media* (Prentice-Hall, 1985), in which we predicted the fusion of video, computer, and telephone technologies; more boxes, buttons, touchscreens, and diskettes later, people were still confused and impatient for the technology to settle down and become standardized. This year, we set up

3

what must be our fiftieth interactive system: an MPC standard CD-ROM player and audio board, a digital video card, and more software on more kinds of disks than we had ever encountered or imagined.

What Is (Are) Multimedia?

Today we call it "multimedia": the computers are faster, the optical discs smaller, and the colors more vivid. But it's still far from a mainstream communication technology. It took us four people, six versions of hardware packages, and untold calls to "help" lines to make our new system work, and clients come to us more confused than ever. Where has this technology come in the past dozen years—and where is it going?

Perhaps we should start with a definition: **Multimedia is a class of computer-driven interactive communication systems which create, store, transmit, and retrieve textual, graphic, and auditory networks of information.** Cynics might say that it's just the computer person's term for what video people used to call "interactive video," while enthusiasts predict that it will become our primary means of communication, instruction, and entertainment. CD-I, DVI, MPC, IVD . . . the alphabet soup goes on with ever more powerful (and incompatible) systems. See Figure 1 for some key definitions.

Figure 1

Multimedia Terms

CBT. Computer-based training, tutorials, and simulations consisting of text and possibly graphics, which provide training by means of a mainframe or personal computer. Also known as CAI (computer-assisted instruction), CAL (computer-assisted learning), or CBI (computer-based instruction).

CD-I. Compact disc-interactive, a CD-ROM based self-contained system which is attached to a regular TV set and displays interactive stills and motion clips, controlled by a simple handset. This standard has been developed and is being promoted primarily by Philips and Sony.

CD-ROM. Compact disc-read only memory, a small optical disc capable of storing and playing back digital data. It is roughly equivalent to about 500 floppy disks in storage capacity.

CDTV. Commodore Dynamic Total Vision, an interactive multimedia player incorporating a CD-ROM player and an Amiga computer engine which can display programs on an RGB or television monitor and which is controlled by an infrared remote control.

Desktop Video. The generic term for video programs which are recorded and edited on small-format equipment including graphics and special effects generated by a personal computer.

DVI. Digital Video Interactive, a standard for compression and decompression of digitized video and audio which is stored on a CD-ROM, digital tape, or large capacity computer hard drive, enabled by specialized cards which are inserted into a personal computer which also controls the flow of the program. This format was developed by GE and RCA and is now sold primarily through Intel and IBM.

Expert System. An interactive program which solves problems or makes recommendations based on users' responses to a set of questions and a "knowledge base" and system of if-then rules. The goal of these systems is to document and provide high-level expertise to novices.

Hypermedia. A classification of software programs which consist of networks of related text, graphics, audio files, and/or video clips through which users navigate using icons or search strategies.

Hypertext. A classification of software programs which consist of networks of related text files through which users navigate using icons or search strategies.

IVD. Interactive videodisc, analog optical discs capable of storing and playing back 54,000 still frames or 30 minutes of motion video (per side) and two channels of audio by means of a videodisc player which can be controlled by a remote control or an external computer. This format has been the mainstay of interactive video for the past decade.

MPC. Multimedia Personal Computer, a trademark for software and hardware systems, which conform to the MPC trade association standards and include support for CD-ROM, digitized audio, and high-resolution graphics in a Windows environment.

PC-VCR. NEC's name for their S-VHS videocassette recorder which can be controlled by a personal computer via a serial cable to support interactive video, video databases, and computer-controlled editing.

PSS. Performance support system, a computer-based point-of-use interactive "job aid" which helps users perform their jobs by providing help, brief tutorials, examples, on-line information, or problem-solving.

QuickTime. Apple Computer's multimedia technology which supports the storage and distribution of motion video, stills, and audio over local area networks.

Teleconferencing. Real-time multi-point communication using voice with still frames or motion video by means of phone lines or satellite broadcasting. This may include multiple channels for two-way phone conversations and transmission of additional computer or graphic data.

Ultimedia. An IBM trademark for their multimedia hardware systems composed of personal computers with CD-ROM players, and optionally DVI digital video capabilities.

Virtual Reality. The display and control of synthetic scenes by means of a computer and peripherals which sense a user's movements, such as datagloves, helmets, or joysticks. These systems allow users to vicariously interact within "virtual worlds."

A New Multimedia Framework

Having defined what is generally considered "multimedia," I propose a framework which goes beyond it—one which attempts to make sense of today's and tomorrow's rapidly merging information and presentation technologies. The Multimedia Matrix (Gayeski, in press) encompasses computer-generated technologies which are ordinarily thought of as "multimedia," but includes systems which are at the lower and higher ends of the continuum of technical sophistication. Furthermore, this model includes "real-time" as well as "pre-packaged" communication systems and their intended uses. See Figure 2.

The Multimedia Matrix classifies communication technologies using two categories: the **bandwidth** (the amount and kind of data a technology is capable of storing, transmitting, or displaying) and the **applications** or intended purpose. Individual systems may provide a capacity for text only, text with graphics, audio, full-motion video, or synthetic images which the user is able to vicariously control. The producers or sponsors of a given multimedia program or system may expect it to provide a means of live, spontaneous, user-generated communications, a conduit for carefully designed and prerecorded instruction, or a way to reduce the need for information and instruction by providing job aids and automation tools. With this model, individual technologies and interventions can be classified more easily, and a broader spectrum of strategies and applications emerges.

For example, text-only applications of multimedia include electronic mail and "help systems" commonly found within computer software. While most information utilities, like CompuServe, rely primarily on text to provide data and messaging capabilities, others, like Prodigy, support color graphics. Performance support tools and expert systems most

Figure 2

Multimedia Matrix
(Gayeski, in press)

BANDWIDTH	<- APPLICATIONS ->		
	inform	**instruct**	**automate**
text	electronic mail		help systems
	information utilities		performance support tools
		hypertext	
graphics			
	audiographic conferencing		expert systems
		CBT	
audio	telephone conferencing		
video		hypermedia	
	video teleconferencing		
		interactive video	
synthetic images			
		virtual reality	V

commonly run on standalone PCs, and so are limited to text and possibly graphics; however, some newer implementations use compressed video and audio to enhance the user interface and provide more concrete information. For example, Intel uses a DVI performance support tool to help quality control engineers to inspect computer chips.

While CBT is, by definition, instructional, hypertext and hypermedia are two information designs which fall somewhere between the categories of information and instruction. Most hypermedia programs are more like encyclopedias and reference tools than textbooks or training manuals, although some implementations include intelligent advisors which guide a user along a focused path of investigation. Others have traditional computer-based testing modules which assess a learner's mastery of content.

Newer multimedia systems are capitalizing upon techniques for compressing video and audio so that they can be "pumped through" phone lines or local-area networks. And so we see new technologies for real-time communication which begin at the relatively simple end of the technology continuum, like telephone conferencing, extend their bandwidth into audiographic teleconferencing and even live motion video conferencing. Systems recently announced by IBM and AT&T, for instance, are turning our computers and phones into the "picture phones," first prototyped several decades ago. Finally, virtual reality promises us the ability to simulate the closest thing to "being there": users may vicariously enter into computer-generated worlds to play, collaborate, or learn.

These systems are not only the products which educational technologists create, but also they are powerful tools which we ourselves can use. For example, electronic information utilities allow subscribers to scan articles, participate in forums, send mail and computer files to colleagues, download shareware programs and graphics from fellow professionals, and book airline seats. We have used these systems to coordinate work with associates and   clients across the globe despite our differences of time and place. Computer-based tools can be used to leverage the experience and time of instructional designers: for instance, we've created a hypertext instructional design tool to aid us in documenting and managing courseware development. A PC-controlled VCR allows us to quickly search for and display clips of our video productions. Telephone conferencing allows a publications committee on which I sit to convene regular meetings among members across three time zones. And last but not least, my five-year-old is enjoying our CD-ROM encyclopedia and a popular video game, "Jones in the Fast Lane," (although I must admit I'm not quite sure what he's learning about life through *that* multimedia experience!).

As we can see from the Multimedia Matrix, many tech-nologies exist in the spaces between categories. Where do we fit electronic mail systems that are used by universities to offer distance education? . . . Interactive kiosks that enable users to dial up to an on-line system to order a product or request further information? . . . An instructional design software system which allows users to develop courseware while accessing on-line tutorials, scan relevant journal articles, and access an expert system on media selection? . . . The image of an intelligent workstation which provides a spectrum of outputs, information, and tools is rapidly emerging. Perhaps the most interesting systems fall between the cracks of our neat models of media and applications, allowing us to alternatively and seamlessly learn about, teach about, and apply new concepts. Not only are the definitions of technologies blurring, but so are our distinctions between communicating, learning, and working. The very foundation of interactivity is a balance of providing and accepting information—a two-way flow which characterizes the essence of communication. New design philosophies and models are required: as Banathy (1992, p. 34) writes, the new "ideal systems design by definition is PARTICIPATIVE. It is design that is carried out by—what I have called—USER DESIGNERS."

This Volume

So, multimedia holds great potential for those who can accept the challenge of constantly changing technologies and who can learn to live on the "leading, bleeding" edge. I am delighted to have been asked to edit this volume on multimedia, and proud to introduce its readers to a very special group of authors—all experienced and respected professionals in these new technologies. The first ten chapters were originally developed for a special edition of *Educational Technology* magazine which was published in May 1992. When we decided to create this book, I added Chapter 11 and an appendix comprised of a set of aids for readers of the volume to use in embarking on their own multimedia projects.

When I invited the chapter authors to write for this work, I asked them to imagine that they were sharing their advice, views, hopes, and frustrations with a close friend. This is not the place, I told them, to "hype" hypermedia nor recount a litany of standard citations. Our task has been to add clarity to what some people now humorously call "muddymedia." In the pages that follow, you'll hear what it's really like to develop, apply, and evaluate multimedia from colleagues who are on the front lines.

David Hon identifies the matrix of skills that are needed in a good multimedia project: through his pioneering work with interactive simulations such as the CPR manikin/videodisc system and his more recent robotic endoscopic simulator, he has learned what it takes to create truly revolutionary experiences.

Bill Whitten and **Pam Knight** teach us how to take promising technology and effective programming and get them accepted within organizations: in Whitten's case, a large business such as AT&T; in Knight's case, state school boards.

The continuing dilemma of which platform to choose is highlighted in **Jim Hoekema's** piece; Hoekema has developed some of the first CD-I programs as well as programs using more standard technologies such as HyperCard, and he compares the two ends of the spectrum.

Leon Murphy from Bethlehem Steel talks about their experiences with another major contender among multimedia standards, DVI.

The most exotic applications, Virtual Reality, are discused by **Sandra Helsel**, one of the leading writers and speakers in this new field.

But multimedia cannot be a tool for the few; we need more developers who are educated broadly in technology, theory, and practice. **William Milheim** presents a model curriculum to do just that.

But what can we expect to gain from multimedia? Two chapters address this fundamental question. **Tom Reeves** shares his conceptual framework for evaluating multimedia: his experience in evaluating major educational, industrial, and military interactive projects over the past decade is second to none. **Christopher Dede** describes the real impacts of which multimedia is capable and places them within the context of his current research projects at George Mason University.

Finally, I have provided some "job aids" for those who have read the preceding chapters and want to get started building teams, identifying and selecting tools, and developing budgets.

Some Conceptual Threads

As an "advance organizer," I direct your attention to a few crucial concepts which thread their way among many of the articles:

- new information requirements, educational environments, and learning theories are drawing our attention to the need for new instructional technologies;
- "multimedia" is an ambiguous technology; we are still struggling for definitions, standards, and effective models;
- "more sophisticated" does not equal "more effective";
- multimedia projects require expertise in diverse artistic, technical, and managerial aspects of the task;
- the true test of any technology is how readily it can be adopted by its intended users.

Although it's easy to get caught up in the brilliant displays and sophisticated design strategies which multimedia systems support, we need to consider how these innovations fit in with the culture of their intended environments. We may complain that those less enthusiastic about adopting multimedia are computerphobic or afraid of change. However, careful examination of diffusion of innovation research points out that people do not resist change; rather they resist the *social* and *political consequences* of change. How does multimedia fit into our current systems? What do teachers do with one computer system and twenty-five first-graders? What do we do with a student who completes a year's worth of biology in three weeks? How are instructors rewarded for developing interactive tutorials vs. writing journal articles or eliciting glowing student evaluations of their lectures?

Aside from communication technologies, our social systems and institutions *are* changing. Participatory decision-making and empowered workforces are replacing layers of management and top-down communication. Attention within educational institutions is being directed toward the development of students' higher-order thinking skills and values rather than the rote memorization of facts. And collaborative and flexible work teams are supplanting the assembly line. What does this mean for educational technologists? It means we need to pay more attention to providing tools and channels of communication among subject matter experts and "empowered" learners than producing our own versions of what we consider "excellent" instructional packages. We need to move faster in creating, disseminating, and updating courseware. We have to realize that there's no one "correct" content or method. We must work with the mainstream technologies that are being used within today's workstations to provide just-in-time performance support. And we need to give up control, letting users be the final "creators" and "editors" of the programs we develop.

Does multimedia work? Technically, yes—although sometimes not without prodding. But does it provide a unique advantage over more traditional communication systems? Some studies have documented substantial benefits. Is it just a set of fancy teaching machines which will be relegated to museums of technology? Many media systems have followed that path. Or is it the inevitable extension of personal computers which will become a part of almost everyone's work/learning/entertainment center? Let's see . . . .

References

Banathy, B. H. Comprehensive Systems Design in Education: Design in Pursuit of the Ideal. *Educational Technology*, 1992, 32(1), 33–35.
Gayeski, D. *The Renaissance Communicator in Information-age Organizations.* Stoneham, MA: Focal Press, in press.
Gayeski, D., and Williams, D. V. *Interactive Media.* Englewood Cliffs, NJ: Prentice-Hall, 1985.

Chapter 2

Butcher, Baker, Candlestick Maker: Skills Required for Effective Multimedia Development

David Hon

IXION, Inc.

To make effective multimedia you need a three-legged stool, a triumvirate, a troika. Strong skills from three very different kinds of contributors will be essential to the success of multimedia as a form of communication, as well as to the success of any individual project. But beware: these skills must be balanced in their influence on a product. For all its glib promises, multimedia has for at least ten years suffered from being dominated by one of three kinds of myopia (which is knowledge and skill turned fanatical).

Business, Artistic, Technical Skills

Let us first observe the three areas of different skills in a multimedia project. It is best that they be viewed as "strengths" on a project, even if the strengths as personified in individuals tend to conflict. To lay these out in a tidy, carry-home matrix, let us say that there are three major reasons to use multimedia. The matrix was developed for a talk at COMDEX on Multimedia in Training, but you can see it would as easily apply to most other multimedia activities as well.

The major reasons to use multimedia in the training situation are:

A. **Condenses Time and Materials.**
   The primary reason for using a number of training technologies is the better use of time and logistics in upgrading skills and knowledge. Most of the business cases are made this way, but the case usually falls short if people don't like it, or if the development and equipment and other expenses prove unwieldy.

B. **Effects Rapid Skills Transfer.**
   Probably a better reason for using good multimedia programs is the rapidity with which a new program (and its contained knowledge and skills) can be implemented. Competition can often be met in the field on a very timely basis if sales centers or branch offices can act rapidly.

C. **Manages Feedback, Evaluation.**
   The best reason may be in the way a computer can track information as the multimedia interacts with the user. We have seen very little of this kind of transactional inter-activity, but it offers the promise of high predictability and consistency in skills transfer.

Other reasons abound, of course, but these should survive the first few cuts. Then, let us call the three areas of necessary skill: (1) **Business**, (2) **Artistic**, and (3) **Technical**, and take a look at how each of the three skills of multimedia development applies to each reason. See Figure 1.

Figure 1

Multimedia Skills Matrix

	BUSINESS	ARTISTIC	TECHNICAL
A. CONDENSES TIME AND MATERIALS	A–1 COST/BENEFIT ANALYSIS: MM VS. CURRENT METHODS	A–2 EMPLOYS "REDUCTION" TECHNIQUES FROM ART, CINEMA, MUSIC, LITERATURE	A–3 STRUCTURES STORAGE AND MANAGEMENT OF DIGITAL OR OPTICAL INFORMATION
B. EFFECTS RAPID SKILLS TRANSFER	B–1 TASK ANALYSIS ON IMPACT OF IMPROVED SKILLS WHEN TRANSFERRED	B–2 CREATES FOCUS, REALISM, AND PSYCHOLOGICAL MOMENTUM	B–3 INTEGRATES STORAGE, I/O, PROCESSING IN ELEGANT SYSTEM
C. MANAGES FEEDBACK, EVALUATION	C–1 DESIGN OF CONTEXT TO PROVIDE MEASURABLE PRODUCTIVITY INCREASE	C–2 ESTABLISHES USER-ORIENTED ENVIRONMENT FOR OPTIMUM BELIEVABILITY, PERFORMANCE	C–3 RAPIDLY COLLECTS, PROCESSES, ANALYZES, DISPLAYS INFORMATION

Knowing full well that matrices can lie even more boldly than statistics, let us now peer into each individual window. Rather than trying to rate the overall importance of one or the other of these skills, let us look at their value in more specific segments of a successful multimedia product.

A. CONDENSES TIME AND MATERIALS

A–1	A–2	A–3
COST/BENEFIT ANALYSIS: MM VS. CURRENT METHODS	EMPLOYS "REDUCTION" TECHNIQUES FROM ART, CINEMA, MUSIC, LITERATURE	STRUCTURES STORAGE AND MANAGEMENT OF DIGITAL OR OPTICAL INFORMATION

A–1. (BUSINESS/CONDENSES)

Through a detailed examination of current methods versus values of multimedia, the Business skill concludes that the proper multimedia approach can save X dollars and X amount of time by providing distributed and individualized course-work, in the form of less time for travel, more consistency and control, and perhaps more timely information online.

Of equal importance will be the Business (managerial) skill of keeping these values paramount throughout the project—when the Artist wants to blow the budget with Hollywood effects, and the Technician wants to place a Mainframe in each of 47 locations.

A–2. (ARTISTIC/CONDENSES)

The multimedia pallette is—as with all pallettes—only as good as the hand on the brush. We tend to forget that through all of recorded history the Artist made continual breakthroughs in communication and human perception. The Artist gave us perspective, which led to maps of a round world. The Artist boiled immense battles onto a small stage. Perhaps of most importance to our A-2 category are the Artist's abilities in "Reduction Techniques."

Reduction Techniques. Then and now, those we call Artists (including writers and video producers) are able to condense and control Time through "Reduction Techniques." Some of these are standard (such as time-lapse in movies and literature), and some are created on-the-fly by each Artist. The ability to use these occasionally requires an Artist to understand the deployment of available technology (i.e., mixing of computer graphics and video).

The reason these Reduction Techniques are important is that they are able to shortcut reality's meandering and waste through the effective manipulation of "representations." We show a still frame of an executive getting on an airplane in Atlanta carrying an overcoat, and in the next still frame we see the executive getting off the plane in New York wearing the overcoat. This took 2/30th of a second in actual time and materials, but look at all the information it conveyed to us. This is not something the Technician knows how to do well because it is "illusion," the antithesis of their starkly honest empiricism. The Business people rarely understand that these techniques spell bottom line results in time and money saved and in effectiveness of the program for the user.

Without these Artistic skills—and there are many more—most multimedia products are doomed to waste and ineffectiveness. "Reduction Techniques" are ways in which an Artist, in one bold perceptual sweep, cuts to our perceptual quick and at the same time saves the immense time and money that a strictly literal approach would require. Of course, these techniques, when in use, are called "intuitively obvious" by the technical people, and "just good execution" by the business people. They should be called *Talent*.

A–3. (TECHNICAL/CONDENSES)

There is an absolutely terrifying range of equipment and technical methodology available to achieve the Business and Artistic objectives. Early decisions on which system to use inevitably revolve around whether you want in the future—increased predictability or freedom to explore new technical options. Ah, yes . . . Freedom or predictability—mankind's perennial dilemma.

When You Haven't Bought the Hardware Yet . . . If you are exploring which equipment set-up to use for your future multimedia projects, you will have a great amount of help from your local equipment dealers. These sales people usually seem to know what they are talking about, but remember that only 1 in 1000 of these people have really participated in a multimedia project of any kind. Your technical people at first may be little better. It is one time when you may be wise to hire an experienced, impartial consultant. They are around. You may wish to find one who has ridden several horses, rather than one who has experience only in computer graphics, or with interactive video, etc.

When You've Already Got a Multimedia Platform . . . If you already have decided on—and purchased—a system, you will have to live with it for better or for worse. This does allow a Technical staff to get in and know the equipment very well. When that happens, this staff can either (1) guard their territory and rule thumbs up or thumbs down on any request of the Business or Artistic factions or (2) be quite creative in structuring storage and managing information and interactivity in the system and be quite alert to ongoing technical additions or modifications that can further enable the basic system.

The group represented by #1 should be fired with all haste allowed by law. The group represented by #2 can create the optimal system, condensing high volume, capability, and speed into a system requiring low cost and low effort to implement.

At their best, they are every bit as creative as any Artist in their quest to achieve an optimal multimedia product. Sometimes their creativity comes in software tricks and sometimes in hardware additions. Sometimes their results are indistinguishable from magic. An important note: these technical people often see themselves as being stoically heroic.

Part of the high-order skills needed by both the Artistic and Business factions will be in "Articulating the Envisionment" to the Technical staff. Often, you have very intelligent people in technical disciplines, who yet have very little empathy with any concerns that evolve only semi-logically from other quarters of the human race (see Spock). Articulation of the Envisionment means creating a clear image of what is desired, and perhaps in time building "empathy bridges" from the Technical staff to the other equally important skills in the multimedia spectrum.

B. EFFECTS RAPID SKILLS TRANSFER

B–1	B–2	B–3
TASK ANALYSIS ON IMPACT OF IMPROVED SKILLS WHEN TRANSFERRED	CREATES FOCUS, REALISM, AND PSYCHOLOGICAL MOMENTUM	INTEGRATES STORAGE, I/O, PROCESSING IN ELEGANT SYSTEM

B–1. (BUSINESS/RAPID TRANSFER)

The purpose of a piece of multimedia is defined by the person who signs the check for its development. In movies, the user finally appears—or does not appear—at the box office. In multimedia games, quarters continue to drop as the user becomes more and more fascinated. In multimedia training, the payoff is that the student rapidly performs, and performs effectively. That's the box office.

But, first of all, someone has to know what performance is needed, or all else is guesswork. The Business function determines what performance is desired. In training, a Task Analysis is made to define what skills will provide the desired results in the real world. Since very few people know exactly why they are successful, this "knowledge engineering" is more difficult than it might seem.

That is why the Business function has to make that judgment. Only when someone makes the commitment to saying what must be conveyed are any of the other functions able to contribute their best efforts.

B–2. (ARTISTIC/TRANSFER)

Whether it is focusing a camera on a foreground, or writing dialogue which exudes character, or bringing in the cymbals in crescendo to heighten a symphony's finale, or reddening cheeks on a painted portrait, the Artist is always there in the best-presented communications. That the "kernel" of importance is found is no accident. That all decisions tend to focus the eye of the beholder on that importance . . . is no accident.

The Artist knows that his job is to focus on the important, and to diminish the impact of the trivial. In multimedia it is just as important as in movies or books, but it is accomplished differently. In the movies and in music, time is a constant. In the photo or painting, space is a constant factor. What you do with the limited time or the limited space you have is what makes the production "work." In multimedia, the time and space available seem almost limitless.

Attention Span as a Canvas. Unfortunately, many multimedia producers act as if the user's attention span is also limitless. But that is the very limitation . . . boredom. Virtually endless selections and branches do not an exciting experience make. It is the grasp of the psychology of the multimedia user, just the same as any Artist's grasp on the fascination of any reader or audience, that makes the product "work." In the case of having a participating spectator, it is the engagement of that person's psychological momentum that makes a multimedia experience "work." And the Artist, in any medium, knows that boring the audience is the only unforgivable sin. There . . . I've said it. Small minds get bored. But even smaller minds do the boring.

The difference in multimedia excitement is in how it is made to respond to the participant. That instant, personal response is more than a reward to the user . . . it is the supreme compliment. People live lives full of deferred response. Tulips don't bloom until spring. Even the incredible idea has to wait for a meeting. And your brilliant performance on the job still waits until review time for its response. But in truly interactive media, your response is *now*. And the quality of that instant response defines the quality of multimedia . . . all else is filler.

The combined quality of the rapid responses in good multimedia is what creates the rapid effectiveness of the experience. The Artist never forgets this for a moment.

B–3. (TECHNICAL/TRANSFER)

If a rich and varied structure of information is to be accessed with screaming precision, the Technical function has to be the system's tireless Pit Crew. It is the Technical group who must figure out how and where to store branches of information. And the next question after "How much information can we store?" is always "How fast can we get to it?"

It is the Technical group who gives the Artist instant response in text, sound, or pictures. It is the Technical group who makes the interactive process totally reliable. So if there is a rapid transfer of meaningful information of any kind to the participant, the Technical group makes the system become the fastest librarian ever, the tireless expert, and the most attentive tutor.

If the Artist is to build a relationship with the user upon personalized, instant responses, the Technical staff must structure the hardware and software for optimal performance. And when the Artist wants to create, the Technician must be there to hand over exactly the right tools.

Truth be known, there are far more tools available in multimedia than Artists who know how to use them. Whose fault that is, is a most difficult question.

C. MANAGES FEEDBACK, EVALUATION

C–1	C–2	C–3
DESIGN OF CONTEXT TO PROVIDE MEASURABLE PRODUCTIVITY INCREASE	ESTABLISHES USER-ORIENTED ENVIRONMENT FOR OPTIMUM BELIEVABILITY, PERFORMANCE	RAPIDLY COLLECTS, PROCESSES, ANALYZES, DISPLAYS INFORMATION

C–1. (BUSINESS/EVALUATION)

If the Business component could simply do its cost/benefit planning, and provide its Task Analysis to the other two functions, it would get exactly what it required: necessary content hopefully in a palatable format.

The irony here is that interactive multimedia is totally capable not only of providing content but also of assuring effective performance with that content. It can set up a valid performance context, monitor every nanosecond of user performance, and feed back incremental results or hints, and it can create a consistent performance profile for every individual user.

The tragedy here is that the Business function rarely asks it to do so. That may be one of the greater wastes in the short history of the Information Age. The fault lies with trainers who are afraid to evaluate the performance of their students—and thereby their own performance. When this generation of artful tappers is given the Business function in creating multimedia, we often still see the same shirking of standards that has made Training the Raggedy Ann of corporate America and U.S. Education the limp roadkill under the wheels of our short-term, bottom-line society.

However, when the Business function hitches up its pants and defines an evaluation of performance for the system to manage—and for the user to achieve—multimedia may have found its true purpose.

C–2. (ARTISTIC/EVALUATION)

In a simulation, it is simple to see that the performance environment must be carefully architected to make sense to the user, and to bear significant resemblance to the real-life situation in which future performance must occur. The Artist's skills in reducing, heightening, and focusing all come into play here because the simulation is truly an illusion. It must seem to be a realistic context, but it does not have to BE realistic. (This is where the literal-minded Technical staff often has problems. They do not deal comfortably with illusion. It is not honest, and it is not honorable: It is not dealing in a real way with stark reality.)

The design of a performance context for the user, however, is not solely the province of "simulation." This very performance context is often called USER INTERFACE. Given that epiphany, it may now be easy to see why the Artist is usually the best designer of the overall environment in which interactive multimedia transactions take place. As we mentioned before, the Artist is most in touch with the "psychological momentum" of the user and with the user's visual perceptions also. And while you are at it, add tactile perceptions and external hardware design. What becomes obvious is that the effective

Artist is always most in touch with the hearts and minds of the audience.

Timing. If there is one factor in all of multimedia where the Artist should be allowed to contribute more, one that is missing in most multimedia and is present in the best multimedia, it is the Artist's fine sense of TIMING. How long do we have to match a sound with a graphic? How long can the system take to respond without the user's mind going on hold? How long are we fascinated by a graphic creating itself on screen, and when do we start tapping our fingers? When, if ever, is motion video absolutely necessary? (With sound and Artistic timing, less than you might think.)

And timing is not all the speed of the technology, either. Remember how Jack Benny got some of his greatest laughs by pausing an inordinate . . . amount of time to reply? These are not tricks. These are the most human of factors.

C–3. (TECHNICAL/EVALUATION)

Remember how dumb you felt the last time you realized you had been assuming that you would have to pay dearly for something that would actually have been free, if only you had asked? Remember how dumb you felt at the last class reunion when a tipsy classmate after whom you had secretly lusted revealed he(she) had always secretly wanted to go out with you, if only you had asked?

That's how dumb you should feel if you have the Technical staff in total control of all data flowing in and out of your multimedia system at a million miles a second, and you don't ask them to collect information through that system.

The mirror image of the presentational and transactional abilities of a multimedia system is its ability to collect information almost effortlessly. If a few extra lines of code are designed in, your multimedia system can collect all sorts of information. Not only to give the users instant feedback and an extremely detailed evaluation of their performance, but also information on how the system itself is working. How many of the users who took over ten seconds to retrieve background information also scored below 70 in the performance profile? How many times was the screen touched in the multimedia exhibit at the trade show? How many users started the program but did not finish it?

What you do with the information can be inspired or wasteful, saintly or downright evil. But the Technical staff can usually enable the system to collect more information than you had dreamed . . . if only you ask.

Conclusion

It should be apparent by now that if any of these skill areas is not appreciated and used to its full potential, the multimedia product will suffer. And yet that is precisely what has happened in the last ten years of multimedia. The Artist has tried to make a painting or a movie out of a participatory experience. The Business person did not have a clear idea of the economies the Artist could actually accomplish, or was bullied by the MIS director into linking mainframes across the world to do text-based courses. Or the Technical staff, obviously the right ones to head up a project, felt that the Artist's palaver about "timing" was all fluff. (Only recently have computer companies discovered that sound goes well with pictures.) Or both the Artists and the Technical staff thought they had unlimited budgets and unlimited time frames with which to complete the project. Or the management had no clear vision of any real result that should come from this thing called "multimedia."

The next ten years will be different.

Chapter 3

The Hurdles of Technology Transfer

William B. Whitten II

AT&T Bell Laboratories

In 1980 I saw a fascinating demonstration of computer-controlled audio-video that illustrated procedures of bicycle repair and showed detailed ballet movements. User control of the images clarified details that were usually difficult to discern and remember. At the time, I imagined widespread adoption of such multimedia capabilities to explain and teach concepts and skills.

In 1980 the technology that could provide randomly accessible audio-video was the laser disc. By 1985, the cost of mastering such discs had improved tenfold, computer graphics had improved dramatically, and several technologies for digitizing audio had become affordable. It seemed that the time had come to embed full-fledged multimedia explanatory systems into the workplace, so we accepted the challenge. Over the next six years we learned much about multimedia technology, but we also learned a great deal about the process of transferring technology from "possibility" to "product." If you set out on this course, you will find a series of hurdles to jump. You will not be surprised to find technical hurdles—some large and some small—but you may be surprised to find many very large hurdles with labels like "sponsorship," "organization," and "timing." In this chapter, I will describe these hurdles and will give advice on how to jump them.

Sponsorship Hurdles

Cultivate Deep and Wide Support. In order to transfer technology from an idea to a product where it is really used, you will need consistent, unwavering high-level sponsorship. Sponsorship means more than just funding: It means that a number of people with the power of the purse believe that what you are doing will have a fundamental effect on the business.

Ideally, sponsorship for your project should be both deep and wide. It should be deep in the organization such that it is understood as far up the hierarchy as possible. In addition to that, sponsorship should be broad. That is to say, a number of people within each level should understand the importance of the work and should be impatient for the work to be completed.

Dependable sponsorship requires that several people in charge of the business and its finances understand the work, want the work, and will pay for the work. It is important to have deep and wide sponsorship because organizations are always changing.

Obtain Simultaneous Support for All Stages. Unless the technology you are dealing with is trivially simple, you will need simultaneous sponsorship for all stages of the project. There must be support for future-oriented work, as well as for the effort that will create a near-term product. When you are working with a new technology, you will need to continually strive to update your product to stay on the cutting edge, and at the same time, you will need to attempt to deliver a completed application that can justify the expense of your work. The best sponsorship, therefore, will be from people who understand the continuum from early work through finished product.

Create a Multi-Year Plan. People are notorious for underestimating the amount of work it will take to achieve success when dealing with new technology. It is not uncommon to miss the estimate by 100 or 200 percent. This difficulty in estimating implies that sponsorship must be flexible and must be willing to commit to multi-year projects. Projects that transfer complex technologies usually require multi-year plans with multi-year funding.

Educate Your Sponsors. Japanese companies are frequently admired for being able to produce new products in amazingly short intervals. We, in American companies, are being pressured to do likewise. By reading case studies of actual products being developed by Japanese companies, I have found that they may have had three-, four-, or five-year development schedules. Apparently, the popular press does not dig deeply enough to discover that the ideas for certain new products go back several years. If they looked into this in detail, they might find that a more important difference between the Japanese development process and the American development process is that key employees in the Japanese corporations stay with their projects from the early concept until the completed product (e.g., Lamm, 1990). I expect that this provides continuity, enthusiasm, and dedication. In American organizations we tend to move people from project to project in short intervals. This fosters a willingness to quickly abandon current work for greener pastures, and generally undermines the development of true expertise. If this is the norm in your business, you will have to educate a succession of sponsors to avoid losing their support.

Calculate Costs and Benefits. One of the most significant but most difficult hurdles to overcome when gaining sponsorship for your project is to justify the costs compared to the benefits. It would seem straightforward that whenever starting any substantial project you should very carefully estimate the costs and enumerate the benefits. As you might imagine, however, if something is truly new, you will only be able to guess what the benefits are. You will not be able to quantify those in strict terms, and you will not even be able to know the real cost until you are deep into the project. The cut and dried mathematical cost-benefit model for making business decisions is mostly fiction when you are working with really new technology. Mainly what you can do is enumerate the potential benefits, put some wild guesses on them in terms of dollars, enumerate the potential costs, and see if it makes sense to take a chance. Ultimately, however, high-level sponsorship must include a vision of the future and a leap of faith by the sponsors.

Organizational Hurdles

Successful technology transfer will cause organizational change. Such change may occur in the producing company, or it may occur in the organizations of the customer that will use the technology, and most likely it will occur in both. To achieve successful technology transfer, you must learn the fundamentals of organizational change, and you must understand the dynamics of the situation you have entered.

A consulting company called ODR Incorporated, based in Atlanta and headed by psychologist Daryl Conners, has developed extensive course work to explain sponsorship and organizational change. Four kinds of players have been identified (Conners, 1991). **Sponsors** are one type of player, and the requirements of sponsorship have been discussed above. The roles of "advocates," "targets," and "change agents" are discussed below.

Enlist Advocates. An advocate is someone who does not have the power to sponsor you, but nevertheless believes that what you are doing is right. An advocate in your organization might be your immediate boss who values what you are doing but does not have the money to pay for it because the money comes from an outside organization or from a higher position in your organization. The advocate can help you achieve your goals by being a consistently vocal and visible supporter and cheerleader. The advocate's role is to assure the continuity of sponsorship by continually looking at the organization as it changes and by making sure that any new people that step into positions are briefed on the importance of the work and are brought into the fold of sponsorship.

Identify Targets. The third group of people affected by the new technology are called "targets" by Conner. Targets are those people who are affected by the new technology whether they want to be or not. If you want technology transfer to be successful, targets are a key group for you to consider because they may be the primary source of resistance to change. Some will have legitimate reasons to worry: Your technology could eliminate their jobs or could cause them to have to undergo extensive changes in how they do their work. On the other hand, your technology may improve the jobs of the targets, and if you are able to explain these improvements, you may find them to be your strongest advocates.

Learn to Be a Change Agent. The fourth class of people identified by the change management experts are called "change agents." If you are advocating new technology to be used in specific ways, you are a change agent. The change agent has the most difficult job because the change agent has to find, establish, and maintain sponsorship. The change agent must educate and retain the interest of the advocates. And, the change agent must be concerned about the effects of the new product—positive and negative—on the targets.

Understand Your Company's Organizations. Sponsors, advocates, targets, and change agents all live in organizations within your corporation. To effect technology transfer, you must understand how your corporation is organized and how the technology that you are advocating will potentially affect each organization. Understanding these organizations requires ongoing, dedicated effort since it is likely that your initial ideas of which organizations will be affected will be far from correct.

I'll use our experiences to illustrate this point. When we started our work, I thought of it as an extension of the user interface that would provide all of the knowledge needed to perform a job in an easily understood and immediately available form. From this point of view, the main organizations affected would be those that develop new systems. Traditionally, however, explanatory information has been subcontracted by the system developers to specialized training and documentation organizations. To achieve successful technology transfer, we have had to work with all three types of organizations. This is a challenging situation because each type of organization has clear goals and budgets to support "business as usual."

Learn Your Way Through the Matrix Management Maze. A common corporate organizational structure consists of a series of parallel hierarchies. Each hierarchy has a clearly stated function, but it is rare when one hierarchy contains all the resources and expertise necessary to create and market a product. This means that these hierarchies are interdependent. When you enter one hierarchy to work on an aspect of a product, you will frequently find yourself loosely linked to another hierarchy that yours is serving or that is serving yours. If you find yourself in this position, you have entered the Matrix Management Maze. Whether or not it is officially recognized as matrix management will make little difference. You will have to recognize where you are and try to find your way out.

The effect of the maze on technology transfer is profound. If you do not find the way out, the maze will kill new technology because it will choke out all forms of change. As far as I can tell, there is only one way out, and that is to bring the top managers of each hierarchy together to form a new team that can make cross-functional decisions and have conjoint responsibility for the outcome. If you cannot do this, you may find yourself in an infinite shuttle between hierarchies.

Master the Hierarchy Hop. On your way out of the Matrix Management Maze, you will need to master the Hierarchy Hop. That is, you need to learn to jump to the level in the hierarchy where decisions and commitments are made. Find the highest level person that you can meet with and the lowest level person who can pay for the work and get those people together. If they like the work, ask them to do some of the necessary follow-up work to assure reliable sponsorship. If they will, you have found the right people and are working with the appropriate levels of your hierarchy.

After you obtain funding, you will need to spread the base of sponsorship and advocacy by showing your work to as many people as possible. When you are obtaining initial support, however, you need to hop to the optimal position in your management hierarchy, because you will not live long enough to present your ideas to all the people who *might* have an interest in your work.

Cause the Necessary Organizational Changes. Once you understand the changes that must occur, try to make them happen. The deployment of multimedia knowledge systems will probably require trainers and technical writers to be brought together into a unified organization with system developers. They will need a new mind-set or frame-of-reference for their work. They will have to learn to write in modular fashion, write scripts for listening, create many more visual elements, and learn some of the multimedia production techniques. They may need to think of themselves as "performance support" experts instead of as writers, teachers, or course developers.

Our work has required us to form cooperative liaisons with training, documentation, work center, and system development organizations. These liaisons are not necessary to develop multimedia capabilities. They are essential, however, to bring about the organizational changes required for technology transfer.

Be Sensitive to the Effects of Your Technology on Its Users. When a new technology is introduced to the workplace, characteristics of jobs will change. A job may be improved, but it also could be eliminated, or it simply could be changed in ways that are not perceived as improvements by the workers.

The American workforce is experiencing massive change. You might imagine that bringing new technology into this kind of environment will cause some people to wonder, "Is this something that will make us less important?" The challenge is to explain your intentions in terms that will make advocates of those who will be affected.

Timing Hurdles

Timing is everything. When you are working on new technology and trying to transfer it to an actual application, you can be too early, too late, or if you are really lucky, just at the right time.

Too Early

Ahead of the Technology Curve. One characteristic of being too early is that pieces of the technology puzzle will be missing. When we were integrating multimedia capabilities with a PC in 1986, we had to use a laser-disc player for audio-video mass storage. This worked fine, but it was very clumsy to update the content. We needed a practical way to store audio and video digitally, but that technology would not become available and affordable until 1990. If you get too far ahead of the technology curve, achieving your goal will be technically difficult and too expensive.

What Is It? If your work is too early, few people will understand what it is and why it is of value. You may find that you are spending far too much time explaining, defining, and selling your work rather than solving technical problems. You may also find limited sponsorship.

Too Many Types of Problems. If you are introducing a technology early, there may be such a broad array of problems to solve that it may not be clear which problems you should work on and which you should leave to others. In our work, for example, there has been work on hardware, software, system integration, user interface design, multimedia production techniques, and authoring procedures. If you are too early, you will not be able to borrow from others' progress, and consequently may find yourself running in too many directions.

Organizational Inertia. Organizational change is usually driven by discomfort with the status quo. This discomfort must rise to a critical threshold so that people are willing to try new things and to look for better answers. Sometimes the pain occurs when the cost of doing things in the old way is too high, and sometimes it occurs when external competitors start to do things in new, improved ways. Without such pressures, the organizational changes that are needed to support your new product are unlikely to occur.

The Chicken and Egg (or Infrastructure) Problem. When you are too early, you may have the chicken and egg problem. You may enter into endless discussions about whether the time is yet right to invest in the technology base. In the case of multimedia, these discussions may take the form of "We don't have applications yet, so we can't spend money on the hardware and software development," or the inverse, "The delivery platform and production techniques are not quite stable, so we can't spend much money to develop an application." This is a common problem associated with innovation, and generically it is the problem of creating an infrastructure to support the new technology. The important realization is that the infrastructure may be more difficult to provide than the technology it supports. Bell invented the telephone by himself, but it has taken thousands of people to create the switching network. Somehow, you have to get out of the chicken and egg problem. I think its resolution is related to the leap of faith that the sponsor must make.

Prototyping Purgatory. Another interesting problem that relates to being too early is what I call "Prototyping Purgatory." Prototyping Purgatory is the state of being constantly caught in prototyping and never being able to go beyond that to make a real product. Prototyping Purgatory may take the form of "make this sample application so that we can show it to customers," but then before you get the sample application completed, some organizational changes may occur, some business priorities may change, or technological advances may outdistance your efforts.

Too Late

Undervalued Skills. Even though you may have begun too early, it is very easy to find that you are now too late. Something may happen in the marketplace that makes what you are doing an order of magnitude easier. If you have worked in the "too early" mode for a while, you will have a background that very few people have, and you will be able to make the right moves to take best advantage of the new technologies. But, if it looks like anybody or everybody can do what you are trying to do, you may not gain full appreciation of your skills.

Premature Standardization. Another problem of being too late in using a new technology is that design innovation may be squelched by premature standards, or worse, by default standards that come about, not through careful study, but simply through use.

Competing Products. Another sign that your application of the technology is too late is that your approach is one of many competing approaches. If your ideas are better and if you have solid sponsorship, this may not be a problem. On the other hand, your progress may be impeded by these competing efforts. They may siphon off funding and other resources, and they may pressure you to make design compromises so that multiple products can co-exist.

Changing Expectations. The product that would have pleased your customer when you started your work may not be acceptable when you have it completed. When you are working on the leading edge, or as it is sometimes called, the cutting edge, you are working with a moving target. Each time you make a decision you are making a risky decision because by the time you get the work finished, new technology may have become available to make what you have done appear old or clumsy. Each time a new competing technology appears, you have to pause and then decide whether it is worth starting over or whether you should finish your product as originally planned. If you complete your originally planned product, it may be eclipsed. If you start over, you may lose sponsorship due to lack of progress. One way to summarize this situation is to say that the cutting edge is not always a comfortable place to be, and sometimes you can get hurt on it.

Just Right

New, but Stable Technology. New technology is often unreliable. It would not be wise to base your new product on the beta-test version of a vendor's technology. Your timing is right if the bugs have been worked out of the technological building-blocks from which you plan to assemble your product.

Developer Community. If you are trying to employ a new technology in a worthwhile way, you are probably not alone. A small user community will exist nationwide, and this community will trade secrets to help each other. Intel's DVI technology, which we have used for full-motion digital video, is a good example of a new technology with this status.

Innovation and Optimization. If your timing is right, you will have the necessary latitude to define user interactions and to work toward an optimal product. This, in turn, will provide the opportunity for creating market differentiation with your product.

Strong Sponsorship. If your timing is right, you will find deep and broad sponsorship. There will be impatience for your finished product, but there will be acknowledgment that some flexibility may be required because you are working with cutting-edge technologies.

Imminent Organizational Change. You should see signs that the organizational changes required to support your product are in progress.

Concept Is Widespread. If your work fits within the framework of a popular new label, your stock may rise. When we started our work, the term "multimedia" typically meant a color slide show with some audio in the background. Now, of course, "multimedia" refers to multimedia computing and includes audio, graphics, animation, and usually full-motion or video-like imagery.

In 1985, when we started our work, there was no label that neatly described what we were doing. About three years ago the term "performance support" came into use to describe work such as ours, and in October, 1991, the first national conference on "electronic performance support systems" was held. We expect that widespread use of labels such as "multimedia" and "performance support" will help us communicate the goals of our work.

This brings me full circle in my discussion of timing, whether too early, too late, or just right. Sometimes you might achieve all three of these. I think that when we started we were too early. What we did was technically difficult. Now the concept behind our work is becoming widespread, and we are on the verge of being too late. The essential novelty of what we are doing, the ability to study the best way of doing it, and the opportunity to create standards are being threatened. On the other hand, if we have proper sponsorship, we are probably "just right" because we have had six years of experience, we have learned through trial and error and hard work many things in the areas that intersect to provide multimedia knowledge systems, and we are now prepared to create systems that can bring a new era of on-the-job learning and self-sufficiency to adult employees in a great variety of businesses.

Conclusion

Technology transfer is the final step toward innovation. It is important to realize that some of the hurdles you must jump are issues of sponsorship, organization, and timing. Careful attention to these issues, as well as to the more obvious technical ones, will greatly increase the likelihood of successful innovation.

References

Conners, D. *MOC Practitioner's Implementation Handbook*. Atlanta: ODR, 1991.

Lamm, J. W. *Miata MX-5 Guide*. Osceola, WI: Motorbooks International, 1990.

Chapter 4

Factors to Consider in Evaluating Multimedia Platforms for Widespread Curricular Adoption

Pam Knight

Texas Learning Technology Group

From evaluation results and from classroom observation, multimedia instructional programs have earned a place in the critical educational environment of today's classrooms. Texas Learning Technology Group (TLTG) began in 1985 with a mission to address problem areas in education utilizing multimedia and to determine whether this form of instruction could make a difference.

Rather than a piecemeal approach, TLTG decided to take a complete curriculum approach to provide everything the teacher and student need for the school year to teach and learn a subject. Our Physical Science course is currently in almost 300 classrooms in 15 states and two countries. We are currently completing our Chemistry curriculum and applying for adoption as a textbook alternative in the state of Texas.

We face many questions in preparation for our next project. With the technology changing so rapidly, we must evaluate a number of factors on an ongoing basis to help ensure product success. This article explores questions to be asked when trying to choose a system for widespread adoption. At present, the answers are not easy. Following are factors we must take into account (summarized in Figure 1).

Figure 1

Factors Involved in Evaluating
Multimedia Platforms

DESIGN FACTORS

Single–screen focus
Graphics and text over video
Motion necessary to teaching
As much video and audio as possible
Large group, small group, individual
    activities
Annual updates
Complex interactive activities

Store and randomize data sets
Mathematical analysis
Collect student data for entire year
Extensive navigation options
Input text and numbers
User selection of very small screen
    areas
Touch screen option

TECHNOLOGY FACTORS

Computing power
Input options
File sizes/compression methods
Computer–based storage capacity
Optical–based storage capacity
Access time
Motion image capabilities
Animation capabilities

Audio capabilities
Video overlay for graphics
Image and audio quality
Quality of on-screen text
Programming/authoring options
Operating system options
Open-ended development tools
Conversion to other platforms

HUMAN FACTORS

User-friendly, easy to use on
  a daily basis
Easy–to–install hardware and
  software

Learning curve/user training
  required
Portability
Packaging

VENDOR FACTORS

Stability of main vendor
Alternate vendor sources
Availability of service

Multimedia philosophy
Development support/tools
Hotline support

COST FACTORS

Total system cost
Number of systems per location
Capabilities for the money
Cost of development

Mastering/duplication/packaging
  costs
Update methods and costs

Design Factors

To target appropriate technology, first we consider instructional design requirements. A simple visual data base of mostly still images or simple animations lends itself to almost any platform. On the other hand, an application requiring complex branching logic based on user input, mathematical data files, and calculations can only be achieved by a system with more computing power.

Our particular needs require complex branching, with data arrays and randomized data sets. We keep records of multiple classes of up to 40 students each for an entire school year. We need to use both keyboard and mouse input, with the additional option of touch input. We believe full motion video is necessary to bring the real world into the classroom and bring the learning process alive. We want large-screen delivery with graphics and video together on one screen. We want lots of navigation options and ways to maximize graphics and programming without getting boxed into a corner. These design factors feed closely into the technology factors.

Technology Factors

For a given project, essentially a platform is frozen for that project, i.e., a decision is made with some assumptions and limitations so that work can begin. But it is always important to consider future growth. Just as the PC of 1982 is no longer adequate for many 1992 needs, the technology of the future will provide new options and more sophistication. So we try to predict the trends. Is digital the wave of the future? Will analog remain a part of the mix? With object-oriented programs and on-screen menus, will TV viewers become computer users?

Technology decisions are driven by design needs. With simulations and mathematical problem solving, our needs are fairly complex, requiring computing power and multiple forms of input simultaneously. We utilize data files in the practice activities, analyze data input, and keep records of individual students and classes.

We use a lot of animation, and we are always stretching the limits of image and audio storage. We want high quality, but we make tradeoffs to keep file size down. We keep text separate from the video images, so it is clearer and easier to update, and so we can position it wherever we need.

It is important to us to streamline our process by reusing graphics and routines as much as possible. But it is equally important to us to have an open-ended development system so we can solve problems, reach into new areas of creativity, and enhance the technology.

We are interested in developing for multiple platforms, but have not yet found that to be economically feasible. Eventually, as all images and sounds become data files, as conversion methods improve, and as vendors cooperate on standards, this should be possible with careful planning.

Human Factors

We can't forget the humans involved. The end-user in our case involves both the teacher and the student—each with different needs. Not surprisingly, students take easily to the computer and are not afraid of a keyboard. But teachers are in a very different position. They must set up the system, figure out how to use it, and handle any technical problems.

We require at least three days of teacher training with our products, to assist teachers in overcoming technology fears and in developing strategies for integrating the media into classroom sessions. But for real success, the system must appear friendly. With a modest learning curve, it must become teacher's best friend for the year. It's there to help, not hinder, on a daily basis.

The search is always for an easy-to-use, easy-to-install, and easy-to-transport system.

For statewide adoption processes, systems must be placed in regional education service centers across the state. Most reviewers will never have viewed a multimedia product before. They must easily peruse this one, just as they would a textbook, to see if it meets the educational criteria established by the state.

Vendor Factors

Day-to-day reliability is a major concern once the system is integrated into lesson plans. What happens if the system breaks down? How quickly and painlessly will it be serviced?

Vendor factors center around the stability of the main vendor and the availability of alternative sources. It's less risky and more competitive to have more than one vendor option for a platform.

We also consider the vendor's overall philosophy and support for multimedia and the education arena. Are they partners in our endeavor? Can we get our questions answered? Are they providing the needed development tools and resources? Will we be able to have input into their future plans?

Cost Factors

Last, but certainly not least, is the bottom-line issue of cost. As technology progresses, the good news is that the cost of the hardware keeps decreasing. And as development tools progress, cost of development promises to lower.

If it were as simple as the lowest-cost platform being the best choice, the decision would be easy. But a lower-cost system may compromise design needs, or may not be as stable, or may not really be so low-cost when all the necessary options are added.

Development is another major cost factor, and the absence of advanced development tools can bring a project to a standstill during development in order to write a program or engineer a solution. When a project begins, it is impossible to know all the requirements, so an important factor is that the tools and process are open-ended enough to handle the exceptions as well as the rules.

Cost of software delivery is affected by mastering and duplication costs. The optical and digital technologies provide alternatives to the mass of floppy diskettes for distribution, but the cost of remastering could make updates more expensive.

Conclusion

It's not easy knowing all the right questions to ask, much less having all the answers. Questions keep arising and answers are many faceted. We will have to lock down a platform for our next project, but for now we are questioning, not answering.

In two to five years, the new DVI, CD-I, and CDTV technologies will shake out. The capabilities, standards, processes, and tools will be better defined and tested by the early developers. But, at present, we are trying to predict a rapidly changing future. I wish us all luck.

Chapter 5

HyperCard and CD-I: The 'Mutt and Jeff' of Multimedia Platforms

Jim Hoekema

Hoekema Interactive

First, let me apologize for alluding to cartoon characters whose memory is almost completely faded from the national consciousness. In fact, I must admit I know nothing about "Mutt and Jeff" except that one was short and the other tall (respectively, I suspect). Somehow, their names persist as a pair of linked opposites—which is how I think of HyperCard and CD-I (Compact Disc-Interactive), the two platforms in which I've had the pleasure of working most during the last four years or so. From my admittedly personal viewpoint, they both represent the promise of interactive multimedia and its challenges—but in different ways.

Comparing the Platforms

Essentially, HyperCard (with videodisc) is a fabulous development platform, but a questionable delivery medium; by contrast, CD-I is a superb publishing medium, but still a rather primitive development environment. Costs associated with each medium follow suit: HyperCard is easy to use, and development is inexpensive, once you have a Macintosh (minimally, an LC with extra memory, for about $2000). While HyperCard-only stacks can be distributed to anyone with a Mac Classic (about $1000), you don't get true multimedia until you use HyperCard to control a videodisc player, which adds another $1000, plus the video monitor, perhaps some audio gear . . . in short, the delivery system can be rather expensive, which reduces the potential market for products in this medium.

By contrast, Compact Disc-Interactive bears most of its costs "up front." The most basic authoring setup, using all Philips equipment or a combination of a development CD-I player and special add-ons for either Macintosh or IBM PC-compatible computers, would cost between $10,000 and $25,000 (depending on what you mean by "basic"). The costs of gathering images, video, and audio will be the same as for videodisc, but the added step of converting to digital format must also be factored in. As a relatively new platform, the software development environment for CD-I still lacks a variety of powerful, easy-to-use authoring tools; skilled programmers are required, and they usually need time to invent a few things in the course of programming an application. As a result, development costs are still high, although they are gradually declining. If an interactive videodisc project, with high production values for a general audience, might typically cost about $250,000, then at this point, a similarly ambitious CD-I program would typically run about $350,000—although several consumer titles have been produced for $200,000 or less.

If development effort is the "bad news" of CD-I, then delivery cost is the good news. After all that hard work, a CD-I program offers a flexible and very rich mix of media, with high-quality images, smooth visual effects, and hours of good-quality audio—all on a handy compact disc, which (if so designed) can play on any CD-I player anywhere in the world, using PAL, SECAM, or NTSC television standards. The non-keyboard point-and-click interface forces a basic level of ease of use. Best of all, the consumer CD-I player lists for $1000 and is widely available for only $800. Compared to anywhere from $4,000 to $10,000 for an interactive video system, that's a significant advantage. The advantages for a market-driven publishing industry are obvious, as is clear from Philips' decision to emphasize the consumer market immediately. But in an organizational setting, such as industrial training, the cost of delivering training (including employee's time "in class" as the largest item) is often many times the cost of developing the course, even in an interactive medium. Thus, what CD-I takes in the development cycle, it more than gives back in the delivery mechanism.

In the following sections, let me describe the particulars of my recent experiences in both CD-I and HyperCard formats.

Example CD-I Product:
"Treasures of the Smithsonian"

Treasures of the Smithsonian was one of the earlier CD-I titles started by American Interactive Media (now renamed Philips Interactive Media of America or PIMA), and it was the first information-based "non-fiction" CD-I to reach initial completion of all media content, in June 1989. That was about two years after we began the project, and the programmers continued to debug and tweak performance for another year. The title was not released, however, until the official unveiling of the Compact Disc-Interactive system (along with two dozen other titles) in October of 1991.

Treasures offers not so much a tour of the Smithsonian as a sampling of the objects, from the famous to the merely typical, held by the 13 member museums and the zoo. Each of the 150 objects is described in a short audio-visual sequence with an often entertaining commentary by *Smithsonian* magazine columnist Edwards Park. Viewers can interrupt presentations to view text notes giving more details, or to "link" to another object (see Figure 1). Some objects also include interactive "toys," which let viewers "walk around" a work of sculpture, zoom in close to a painting, or "play" an African thumb piano, to mention a few examples. Viewers choose which presentations to view from several alternate paths (by museum, category, alphabetical list, historical timeline, or thematic

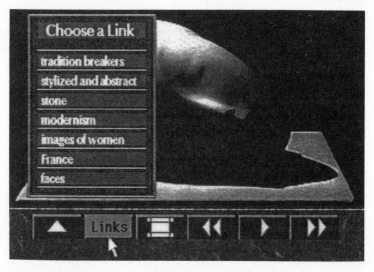

Figure 1. A typical treasure, with Links menu, from *Treasures of the Smithsonian.*

tour)—represented metaphorically as objects in a great hall vaguely reminiscent of Smithsonian castle (see Figure 2).

Treasures is extremely easy to use. There have been no reports of people not understanding how to make selections or navigate the program, which was among the five top-selling CD-I titles during the Christmas 1991 season. The user interface is simple and obvious—but achieving this simplicity took a lot of hard work! The development team consisted of the following: the designer/producer or project director; an "outside" writer (Ted Park); an "inside" writer/editor, who formatted Ted's text into storyboards (Mike Nibley); a full-time photo researcher for a year (Juliana Montfort); a full-time audio researcher and producer, who located music and sound effects and directed the narration recording sessions (Mark Phinney); a general production assistant, who directed image capture and maintained the database (Amy Hough); the lead programmer (Jon Singer) and some additional programmers for various

Figure 2. The Main Hall (main menu) of *Treasures of the Smithsonian.*

components; and several graphic designers, including a model-making firm (Taylor Made Images). Given the early stage of CD-I when we were working (release 1.0 of the operating system came about halfway through), everything required a little more work than it would if we were to do another one today. But the result is a well-produced program with a sophisticated, easygoing quality, about objects of broad cultural interest to many people. Until the advent of CD-I, this kind of general-interest, cultural program could only have been produced for an exhibit. Now, a rich multimedia experience can be had from a department store for $50!

Example HyperCard Product: National Geographic "Rain Forest"

The National Geographic Society publishes educational products in several interactive media. The *Mammals* program, on CD-ROM for IBM PCs and compatibles, is one of the best-selling titles in this medium. A second program in this format, on *American Presidents*, was released early in 1992. The videodisc program initially published as simply *GTV*, on American history, consists of two videodiscs and software for any of three platforms: Apple II, Apple Macintosh, or IBM PC and compatibles. After selling well to schools for about $1000, the program now has a sequel, called *Planetary Manager* (on the environment), with software developed by LucasArts and video produced by Colossal Pictures.

When asked about creating software to make use of the National Geographic Society's extensive library of existing material, I proposed a format that has now become a third product line, called "STV." The first title in the STV series, *Rain Forest*, was released in December 1991 (see Figure 3). Unlike GTV, which represents all-original production, the idea behind the STV series was to re-use existing media—not only films and

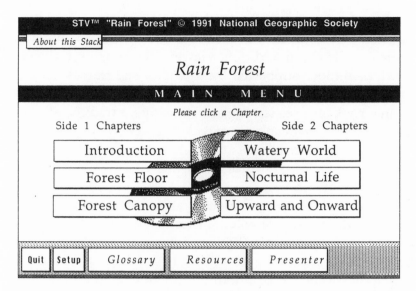

Figure 3. Main menu of the *Rain Forest* program.

television specials, but also filmstrips, books, and magazine articles.

The *Rain Forest*, intended as a school product for grades 6–12, consists of a videodisc and a pair of HyperCard stacks. The main stack features six chapter menus, each with 3 to 7 topics, which give access to the segments of the original film, a beautiful work emphasizing rare shots of the wildlife in the rain forest in Costa Rica. Clicking on "Scripts" brings up the script of the relevant portion of the film. Before viewing, teachers can show Preview Questions—advance organizers for students to anticipate the contents of the video segments. Afterwards, teachers or students can take the Review Questions, with multiple-choice answers and feedback. As "enrichment" rather than core curriculum, the questions in STV have an informality designed to extend learning rather than measure performance. For example, sometimes two or even three out of three answer choices may be correct. Feedback usually includes a short video segment. Sometimes the questions are visual, as in "What animal is this?" In addition, viewers can consult a glossary (with definitions supported by videodisc still frames), or read an article from the *National Geographic* magazine or a chapter from a book on a related subject. Filmstrips, a traditional staple of educational publishing, are recycled here as "photo essays" with great success: students or teachers can read the short text snippets on the Macintosh screen while viewing the visuals on the video monitor.

The second stack, the Presenter, allows students or teachers to create their own presentations (see Figure 4), working from lists of video segments (broken down into small units of 10 seconds to a minute) and still frames. (The still frames are duplicated at the identical frame addresses on both sides of the disc, so users need not worry about which side is up when

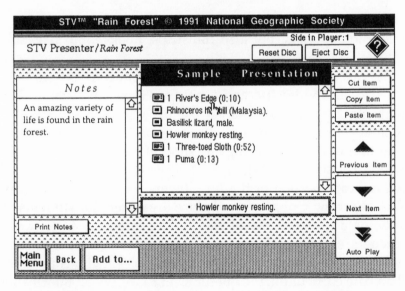

Figure 4. A typical student presentation from the *Rain Forest.*

using still images.) These presentations can be saved and edited, so that many individuals can keep "shows" for later use. To run the presentations, users can use an "Auto Play" button, select them one by one, or advance them by a "Next" button— probably the most practical scheme for a classroom presentation.

Essentially, only two people produced the *Rain Forest*. The producer (Meryl Moskowitz) coordinated the effort within National Geographic; selected the films, articles, book excerpts, and filmstrips; and supervised the transfer of the original video material and photography to videodisc. The designer/scripter (this writer), designed the interface, scripted the HyperCard stacks, and wrote the questions and feedback. We worked collaboratively, over several iterations, to define the segments, name the clips and photos, write the "helps" and directions, and arrive at the final design for the "Presenter" section. Support services included a staff editor, who checked for errors and consistency, and the Geographic's "publication arts" department, which provided the half-dozen maps used to illustrate the magazine articles.

The task of "repurposing" existing material is more complex than it seems, and adding almost 300 stills to the program requires some expensive time in the editing studio. Nevertheless, the production costs were fairly modest, thanks to the great advantage of starting with already produced material of high quality. (The STV product is priced at less than a third of the all originally produced GTV line.) On the software side, development for *Rain Forest* cost a small fraction of that for *Treasures* (including original tool development), but the market is smaller, so the retail cost is higher (about $280), and end-users must spend at least $3,500 on a Mac, a videodisc player, and a monitor. (Another point to keep in mind is that students can produce and store their own creations on the Macintosh—not to mention using the computer for other purposes—whereas the CD-I consumer player is strictly a read-only device.)

Future Prospects

The future for HyperCard and CD-I seems "cautiously optimistic," but the reasons for both the optimism and the caution are different for each platform. The future of CD-I is an enormous gamble, on which the Dutch electronics giant Philips has "bet the store" after a couple of years of disappointing earnings. On the whole, I think it's a good bet. The system offers a truly rich mix of media—admittedly still lacking full-screen, full-motion video, scheduled for addition and upgrade later in 1992. But even without full-motion video, the mix of media and interactivity at a cost of $800 per delivery station is simply unbeatable. (Commodore's CD-TV offers an inferior media mix for the same price.) Besides, CD-I is a world standard, and many other manufacturers will be introducing other brands of players later this year—including Sony's delightful portable model.

At the same time, the growth of this market will be slower than it might be in a booming economy, and the fundamental novelty of the interactive medium awaits a "monster hit" application that will drive player sales the way the original spreadsheet "Visicalc" got the personal computer industry rolling.

At one time, HyperCard's future seemed a shoo-in, because it was bundled with every Macintosh sold. That was good, because it's hard to sell a program that performs such an idiosyncratic set of functions as HyperCard does. Now that the product has been turned over to Apple's software subsidiary, Claris, it seems to have stalled. Claris doesn't quite know what to do with it, and developers can no longer assume a common platform for publishing black-and-white interactive demos and how-to stacks.

HyperCard is by far the fastest tool for creating interactive presentations. It is still the perfect "sketch medium" for other interactive media (we used it extensively in developing *Treasures*). It is also an excellent software platform for controlling videodiscs, especially with the drivers and tools published by the Voyager Company (Santa Monica, CA). But there is a chance that HyperCard will lose its "mainstream" status and become more of a specialist's tool. If that happens, it will be a shame, since viewing HyperCard stacks is a great way for more and more people to understand the nature of interactivity.

Only one thing is certain: interactive multimedia is here to stay. All fields of human communication can benefit from the high information-bearing capacity combined with the time-saving, individualizing interactivity of the merged media. Ten years from now, we may all still be using HyperCard, CD-I, both, or none of the above—but we will certainly be communicating through interactive multimedia.

This chapter is based on a talk given by the author at the Media 92 Conference in Los Angeles, February 27, 1992.

Chapter 6

DVI in Organizational Information Retrieval and Training

Leon A. Murphy

Bethlehem Steel Corporation

The DVI (Digital Video Interactive) multimedia technology, in partnership with computerized information availability, offers a significant opportunity for organizations to enhance employee and organizational performance. As organizational entities commit to quantum changes in their business processes—within the concepts of (in one industry or another) Reengineering, Business Process Improvements, Total Quality, Organizational Retooling, Lean Production, Market Driven Quality, and Agile Manufacturing—closing the learning loop with information and training on demand, within a just-in-time job context, becomes critical to success.

For many organizations, DVI, with its friendly and effective interface to information and training systems, can be a keystone in building the bridge to get from where they are today to where they must be in the future in order to be competitive, successful enterprises.

Multimedia Training at Bethlehem Steel

Interactive computer-based multimedia training systems have been in use at Bethlehem Steel since 1986. This training approach has been effective using videodisc technology, which has established a base of interactive systems. DVI has emerged in the natural progression of the technology supporting interactive learning. Its networking capability, greater flexibility, and increased capacity for audio, video, graphics, animation, and simulations all provide a new base for providing training on demand. This technology can provide powerful front ends to data and information retrieval packages. These new capabilities permit employee learning within an actual job context. They help to facilitate the empowerment of employees by providing tools for using information effectively.

In the past decade, Bethlehem Steel has moved from a low-tech to a high-tech enterprise. Of particular importance in this shift has been the need to keep the work force in step with changing technologies. New employees must be able to meet challenging skill requirements, particularly the ever-increasing computer skills needed by process manufacturing and marketing systems.

Bethlehem is now looking at ways to help ensure a smooth transition from today's to tomorrow's work force. Several areas are critical as the company prepares for the changes in the work force in the next 10 years. There is a need to keep the skills of our existing employees up to date to allow them to better use available and upcoming technology. There is also a need to better motivate employees to improve their job performance

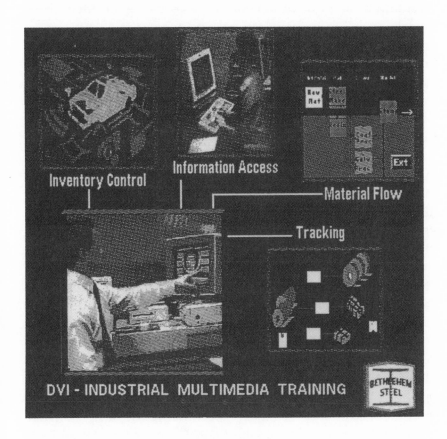

and skills. It is essential to provide information and training on demand that employees require in order to do their jobs.

Interactive computer-based multimedia training is a key methodology the company has used to help upgrade the skills of employees and to keep these skills current with the latest technological developments. An ongoing challenge of operating new computerized systems is training employees to use them properly. Interactive training helps by enabling education and training to be done in bite-sized pieces as part of the normal workday. This greatly reduces problems, such as loss of productivity, often associated with training programs that require groups of workers to leave the work place for training sessions.

Benefits of Multimedia-Based Training

The interactive computer-based multimedia training programs of today consist of multimedia modules programmed in logical-access scenarios. Multimedia consists of still photography, motion sequences, music, voice, graphics, text, and animation under computer control. In addition to training in technical and human resources, the courses provide expert assistance modules, simulations for practice exercises, glossaries, short video sequences of management perspectives, and motivational themes. They also include tables of contents and indexes for quick reference.

Zero travel time, flexible scheduling, self-pacing, high retention, continuous availability, and a non-threatening learning environment are all positive benefits of this technology-based learning. In 1992, over 100,000 hours of interactive computer-based multimedia training will be completed within Bethlehem Steel Corporation. Over 7,500 employees so far have completed at least one interactive computer-based multimedia course. Since 1987, some employees have completed 15 to 20 of the 100 courses that have been offered.

There are four primary goals of the present interactive computer-based multimedia training programs:

- To stress to employees as part of a company-wide effort the critical importance of product and process quality, and to carry out quality upgrading in all operations.

- To contribute to personnel upgrading efforts.
- To provide initial and refresher training.
- To boost employee morale, self-esteem and motivation, which help sustain a self-driven, self-scheduled, self-paced, and self-directed lifelong learning program.

The types of instructional methods used are varied according to the particular needs of the application being considered. These include using short presentations on concepts; using graphics and animation to illustrate a point; and using still pictures and video sequences and explanations. There are opportunities to practice an activity and self-administered quizzes to measure understanding or proficiency.

Interactive computer-based multimedia training involves the user with the material presented. Provisions in the design allow for the multimedia training to be used by several different training populations (for example, supervisors, workers, and salespeople). There are a variety of paths that users may take through a program. By providing for selections and options throughout a program, each trainee can make choices which provide a degree of individualization to best fit that person's needs. However, when required, the computer program can exercise control and move the user to view specified segments of the program (to meet federal safety requirements, for example).

Employees often do not have time to take one- or two-week classroom cram courses. Individualized training in a corporate classroom environment is usually very limited, because the instructor does not have enough time to ensure that each student has mastered the information. Also, the business often suffers when groups of workers leave the job for training. However, by individualizing computer-based multimedia interactive learning and by spreading the training out over time, very effective ongoing training can be done with minimum impact on everyday business operations.

Employee Acceptance

The acceptance of interactive training by employees has been very high. In many cases, a reluctance to take training courses has been replaced by an active push to get scheduled on the terminals to complete additional courses. In several locations, the availability of interactive training has proved to be a morale builder. Employees feel that they are deriving a great benefit from the availability of these training programs. The interactive training stations are located in Learning Centers at various plant locations. However, in certain high-need areas, the training stations are placed right at the work sites. Most of the interactive training takes place one-on-one, although in some instances team training is used on a training station.

While the initial cost of an interactive computer-based multimedia training program is higher than the development of classroom training, the cost-benefit results can be dramatic. Tests have strongly indicated that retention of the interactive training material is much higher than that obtained via classroom training, and up to 40 percent reduced training time has been achieved. The material presented is consistent, and it is available for review or refresher whenever the business is open.

From a management viewpoint, it has been demonstrated that interactive computer-based multimedia learning is a key way to get employees to use company business process systems and standard operating procedures correctly. Company expertise is marshalled to collect key information, and it is incorporated into high-level, interesting, and consistent training programs. If something is wrong, it can be corrected, and all employees immediately have access to correct information.

The latest educational concepts call for instruction that is self-driven, self-scheduled, and self-paced. Fast learners can go through the material quickly and return to the job. Slow learners can travel through the material at their own pace, not holding up others, and not appearing inadequate in front of their fellow employees. This type of learning is excellent for teaching workers how to access and navigate through information in a non-linear way.

Advantages of DVI Technology

Bethlehem Steel has established a strong base for computer-based multimedia learning. This base provides a good platform for the company to move in more innovative uses of technology-based learning, which the DVI technology exemplifies. The new Action Media II boards offer improved real time video, which eliminates the need for outside compression for many applications. Changes are also easily made. The video windowing capabilities are effective. A time-based corrector is not needed. The video show-through with graphics overlay provides for improved video resolution. The Action Media II boards can co-exist with other video boards, such as M-Motion, in the same computer platform. This allows for both videodisc and DVI material to be operated from the same system. LD-ROM players will improve versatility. The networking capability of DVI offers a wide range of potential for future applications, and the large amount and variety of rapid-response information that can be called up directly from a menu screen is impressive. Random-access to multimedia information and desktop delivery are also key DVI capabilities.

An Example

A recent project using the DVI technology has proved to be very successful. This project, "Interactive Training for the Automotive Industry Segment Model," is a presentation system, a sales system, an information system, an instructional business process system, and a detailed training system. The 8

1/2 hours of interactive instructional material, available from a menu, supports the marketing and training requirements for computer mainframe business system applications in the automotive and metals industries. The mainframe computer applications and the supporting DVI interactive computer-based multimedia material operate in a multi-company environment and will support a large number of future users. It appears likely that this type of approach will be used widely in the future to support the high-performance use of computer applications in industry and in the public sector as well.

Conclusion

The availability of DVI computer-based multimedia information and training capabilities phases in with the new needs of business organizations. The quantum changes within business processes must be supported by equivalent changes in information and training support mechanisms. Good enough is no longer acceptable.

All of America and the world are in a period of challenge and change. Improved learning will be a major factor in accomplishing successful organizational transitions. Technology-based learning, if properly managed and implemented, could become a very positive and effective organizational and personal development tool for the future. DVI is one of the key technologies that can help to accomplish this.

Suggested Readings

Bowsher, J. E. *Educating America: Lessons Learned in the Nation's Corporations.* New York: John Wiley & Sons, Inc., 1989.

Gery, G. J. *Electronic Performance Support Systems: How and Why to Remake the Workplace through the Strategic Application of Technology.* Boston: Weingarten Publications, 1991.

Hammer, M. Reengineering Work: Don't Automate, Obliterate. *Harvard Business Review*, July–August, 1990, 104–112.

Harrington, J. H. *Business Process Improvement: The Breakthrough Strategy for Total Quality, Productivity, and Competitiveness*. New York: McGraw-Hill, Inc., 1991.

Rosen, R. H. *The Healthy Company: Eight Strategies to Develop People, Productivity, and Profits*. Los Angeles: Jeremy P. Tarcher, 1991.

21st Century Manufacturing Enterprise Strategy: An Industry-Led View, Vol. 1; *Infrastructure*, Vol. 2. Iacocca Institute, Lehigh University. Bethlehem, PA: 1991.

Womack, J. P., Jones, D. T., and Roos, D. *The Machine That Changed the World: The Story of Lean Production*. New York: HarperCollins, 1990.

Chapter 7

Virtual Reality and Education

Sandra Kay Helsel

Introduction

As a profession, education is responding powerfully to the notion of virtual reality curriculum. Educators seem to have an instant—and almost visceral—understanding of the learning potential that well-designed, virtual experiences could offer students.

The public media, however, have charged the discussion about virtual reality to such an extent that it is necessary to stress that serious technological and research questions must be answered before virtual reality is meaningfully available to any profession, including education. In fact, the majority of widespread end-user applications will not be available before 18 months and maybe as long as five years from now. As for educational research for virtual reality curriculum, the theoretical agenda is not yet even framed at this time.

73

Just what are the educational promises of virtual reality? Will virtual reality allow educators to act as gods—creating new realities and magical worlds with educational Utopias where all students learn? It is the purpose of this article to provide a basic understanding of virtual reality from an educational perspective in order that readers can move to seriously address the educational issues as the research data and technologies mature. Briefly, this article will describe:

(1) the debate between conceptual and technological orientations to virtual reality;

(2) the conceptual orientation to VR;

(3) the technological definitions of virtual reality, artificial reality, and cyberspace;

(4) dimensions of virtual reality; and

(5) virtual reality's impact upon education.

Concept Vs. Technology

There is a great deal of confusion—and rich debate—over the exact "meaning" of virtual reality, artificial reality, and cyberspace. Fundamentally, the division is between a conceptual orientation to virtual reality, artificial reality, and cyberspace versus a technological orientation.

Social psychologists believe that meaning is constructed by groups within cultures who create frameworks for consciousness—frameworks which rely on common, shared symbols and representations. Many of those with a technological orientation to virtual reality have a vested economic interest in seeing VR defined in terms of their specific products. Unfortunately, over the past year, the public media have done a great deal to further the technology-only vision of virtual reality (specifically in terms of headgear, fiber optic gloves, and arcade war-games).

But the concept–versus–technology debate is important—especially to educators. For it's quite different to regard virtual reality as a mental phenomenon which can be orchestrated (via certain technological configurations) rather than regarding the technology(ies) as the most important element in virtual reality. In the conceptual orientation, the "human" processes (whether cognitive, social, emotional, spiritual, etc.) of the student are the focus of the designer, and the computer becomes merely a tool for expediting or replicating a process that causes the user to become a participant in an abstract space. Conversely, when the technology becomes the primary focus, the emphasis is placed upon the mechanical, i.e., software capabilities, system architecture, eye physiology, etc., rather than upon the student.

Habermas (1971) pointed out that any technology is invested with ideological orientations. Today's debate over virtual reality's "meaning" (conceptual versus technological) is literally a battleground between two unique value configurations.

Each educator will have to decide which of the orientations he or she honors—and while this article is unashamedly biased for the conceptual orientation, it provides information about the technologies as well.

The Conceptual Orientation

Virtual reality is a process that enables users to become participants in abstract spaces where the physical machine and physical viewer do not exist.

Historically, humans have been seeking "virtual reality"-like experiences throughout our species' existence. We seem to have an innate ability to seek out experiences that transcend the normal, everyday world. Glimpses of artificial experiences can be seen in literature such as *Alice in Wonderland* or the *Wizard of Oz*. In fact, a spellbinding movie can cause the viewer to become mentally lost in "another world," but that viewer does not have the ability to influence the events or inhabitants of that world.

Only most recently have humans been able to interact with artificial worlds via simulations or expertly designed multimedia programs. For the future, it will not only be possible for a user to interact within virtual worlds as her very own persona, but also it will be possible for that user to mentally become another person—much as Sherry Turkle predicted almost ten years ago in the *Second Self* when she wrote of new technologies: "You inhabit someone else's mind. . . You are Scarlett O'Hara, opening the door to Tara. You are Rhett Butler, deciding to stay rather than leave" (Turkle, 1984, p. 78).

Definitions of the Technologies

The term "virtual reality" is currently used to describe an extensive gamut of technologies. Within the genre, there are further semantic and technical breakdowns—including virtual reality, artificial reality, and cyberspace. Distinct differences distinguish the various categories of technologies, i.e., artificial reality configurations are not tethered and do not include cables linking the user to the computer, such as in the case with virtual reality systems.

This section shall briefly describe the three major types of technologies and their chief characteristics.

Virtual Reality. From a technological standpoint, virtual realities may be seen as a form of human-computer interface characterized by an environmental simulation controlled only in part by the user (Spring, 1991). Additionally, virtual reality requires hardware and software that furnish a sense of: (1) inclusion (immersion), (2) navigation, and (3) manipulation.

As popularly defined, a virtual reality computer configuration consists of a hardware combination that minimally includes a headmounted display, a dataglove, and a tracking device. The viewer wears the headmounted display that contains sensors to track the position of the x, y, and z three-dimensional coordinates of the head as it moves. The viewer also wears a dataglove which provides hands-on interaction with the virtual world. To do this, the dataglove registers finger and hand gestures using fiber-optic cables that act as sensors to detect fingers flexing, while an electromagnetic sensor locates the glove's position in space. Together, all sensors report the positions of the goggles and glove to a computer. The computer then calculates what the artificial world looks like from that angle, draws it in 3-D, and shows it on the LCD screens mounted in the headset in front of the user's eyes.

Artificial Reality. Artificial reality can be described as an interactive environment that emphasizes unencumbered, full-body, multi-sensory participation in computer events (Spring, 1991). Myron Krueger, often referred to as the grandfather of "artificial reality" and who coined the term in 1974 for his doctoral dissertation, describes artificial reality as "graphic worlds that people can enter from different places to interface with each other and graphic creatures" (Krueger, 1991).

Krueger's Videoplace is probably the world's best known artificial reality exhibit. Participants of Videoplace have their live video images manipulated (moved, scaled, rotated) in real time and displayed on a large screen in front of the viewer. Krueger's interactive environments emphasize unencumbered, full-body, multi-sensory participation in computer events. In one example, a sensory floor detects participants' movements around a room. A symbol representing the user moves through a projected graphic maze that changes in playful ways if participants attempt to "cheat." In another, participants can use the image of a finger to draw on the projection screen.

Cyberspace. This is a place where the human nervous system and mechanical-electronic communications and computation systems are linked (Spring, 1990). Cyberspace originated in the writings of William Gibson:

> A consensual hallucination experienced daily by billions of legitimate operators, in every nation, by children being taught mathematical concepts... A graphic representation of data abstracted from the banks of every computer in the human system. Unthinkable complexity. Lines of light ranged in the nonspace of the mind, clusters and constellations of data. (Gibson, 1984, p. 51)

Cyberspace as an educational medium is already being explored by such visionaries as Joseph Henderson, M.D., of the Interactive Media Laboratory at the Dartmouth Medical School. He developed a rudimentary cyberspace program for Vietnam War wound data in which data and information are presented geometrically. This presentation style facilitates the handling and accessing of large quantities of information that make it possible to view highly qualitative information almost directly, while preserving the quantitative. Henderson provides a glimpse of the educational future of cyberspace when he writes that cyberspace can be used to "... promote understanding, augment our ability to process information into knowledge, and perhaps so achieve some wisdom." (Henderson, 1992, p. 22)

Dimensions of Virtual Realities

In a landmark essay entitled "Informating with Virtual Reality," Spring set forth an important paradigm which incorporates the three independent dimensions of any virtual reality program. Although Spring did not specifically propose his paradigm for education, it can be utilized for those who want to understand, design, or use virtual curriculum. Within his paradigm, Spring described three variables of virtual reality—each with their respective continuum. Those three are: (a) user's level of control; (b) nature of the reality base; and (c) naturalness of the interaction. These dimensions are discussed briefly.

Control. A continuum of control will be available for the designers and users of virtual reality curriculum. At the lowest level of computer control, the student (or the teacher) will be in complete control of the system and the program. Further up the control continuum, VR with artificial intelligence capabilities will be able to respond independently of the student—perhaps based on previous input or existing database information. At the most extreme end of the control continuum, the virtual reality system will assume control and will not accept instructions from the learner (or instructor), i.e., as the computer Hal assumed control in the movie *2001*, or as the Holodeck's computer seized control on certain "Star Trek" episodes.

The notion of control has provided serious and intense anger in the professional cyberspace community. At one end of the continuum, certain groups believe cyberspace should be developed without constraints in real-time by each viewer as he/she pleases. Further along on the control continuum are design theorists who believe cyberspace should have certain rules and hence certain levels of control. An example of a well-known set of control principles for virtual reality programs is presented herein, to introduce educators to the kinds of deliberation currently taking place in the professional cyberspace community. Michael Benedikt of the University of

Texas has proposed these "Seven Principles of Cyberspace Design":

(1) **Exclusion.** No two objects may be in the same place at the same time.
(2) **Maximum Exclusion.** In every successive embedded world there are fewer data points than the world that includes it.
(3) **Indifference.** The world is indifferent to a user.
(4) **Scale.** Motion through a cyberspace takes place at a rate inversely proportional to the complexity of the space through which it occurs.
(5) **Transit.** Movement must traverse intervening space and involve some cost.
(6) **Personal Visibility.**   One may not enter a space invisibly.
(7) **Commonality.** The bandwidth of communication between two people in cyberspace is a function of the size of the overlap of their world.

Currently, control issues about virtual reality are predominantly being debated in the computer science community. Educators, who may not be aware of the debate—or may come late to the discussion—need to be aware that a control continuum does exist and can be programmed into virtual reality curriculum.

Nature of the Reality. The second dimension of Spring's paradigm is a continuum describing the type of reality portrayed. At one end of the continuum, virtual reality software can present computer-mediated realities. Further along on the continuum are the simulations of actual reality; and at the far end of the continuum are the computer-developed alternate realities that suspend the laws of our universe.

Computer-mediated reality systems are those wherein the user interacts with the computer's interface in one location, but the commands are enacted (perhaps via robot) in a second location. Well-known uses of computer-mediated reality systems would include remote-controlled undersea or interplanetary robots. In an educational setting, students could interact with the controls of such a VR system in a "homebase" classroom, but a remote robot would perform the corresponding action (experiments) in a distant—or hostile—environment.

Further along the continuum is the replication of a reality that is possible but not actual. In other words, the data source is based in reality—but it is not really happening. For example, VR curriculum could be constructed that accurately duplicates experiences in a foreign country. Students could "travel" via VR to the foreign country and interact with artificial agents for the purpose of learning a language. An actual location forms the basis for such a visualization; but the student experiences a reality that could be—but is not actually—happening.

At the extreme end of the reality continuum are computer-developed alternate realities. In these microworlds, laws that govern the known universe can be modified, suspended, or contradicted by the system's user. Stuart (1991) describes a physics class in which students using virtual reality curriculum create alternate worlds that violate physical laws of our universe. Stuart's hypothetical physics students do not work out problems on paper, but rather create cyberspace worlds in which they tinker with physical forces such as gravity. They learn via their experimentation that changes in gravity can be compensated for by fluctuations in other areas—such as fluctuations in atmosphere surface-to-volume ratio. Younger students in Stuart's hypothetical example become imaginary cyberspace creatures whose physical bodies must change when the gravitational forces of the artificial world fluctuate. To extend upon the example, the older physics students create and manipulate abstract symbolic representations of mathematical principles and formulae.

Naturalness of the Interaction. The third dimension of Spring's virtual reality paradigm is a continuum that establishes the naturalness of the user's interaction with the program.

At the lowest level, the user's physical motion is not equivalent to the natural physical motion, i.e., as a cursor or a desktop mouse movement input is not truly equivalent to body movement. However, because of its low cost and use of already extant technology, this low level of "naturalness of interaction" may be the first type of VR interaction that reaches classrooms. Such kind of input can already be seen in the use of the mouse for rudimentary VR programs on the Macintosh.

Further along on the "naturalness of use" continuum are today's working VR projects where users are tethered by devices such as eyephones and datagloves. With these systems, pointing causes the user to "walk" or "fly" through the artificial world. But, regardless of the movement, it must be remembered that these hand motions do not truly replicate reality.

At the furthest end of the "naturalness of interaction" continuum are the use of natural body movements—*sans* electronic tethers. For example, in "Star Trek's" Holodeck, natural body movement takes place and is computer-read. Concomitantly, the system's response is completely indistinguishable from reality. The upper end of the naturalness continuum will be the last to be developed for common usage due to the massive technological barriers to its implementation.

Virtual Reality's Impact Upon Education

Virtual reality will bring about at least two major changes in the educative process. Learning via printed symbols in textbooks will shift to learning via simulations. Secondly, curriculum materials will no longer be predominantly text-based, but will be imagery and symbol-based.

Virtual reality has the potential to move education from its reliance on textbook abstractions to experiential learning in naturalistic settings. For example, rather than reading about an historical event, students could participate in the event and interact with simulated persons from that historical era.

The creation of these experiential types of virtual reality curricula will raise profound questions from all quarters—and is the basis for numerous future studies. How does one ethically and accurately depict another time, and recreate a once-living human being? Historians, psychologists, anthropologists, educators, etc., must all come together for the creation of these realistic microworlds.

Virtual reality has the potential to move education from its reliance on written text to a reliance on imagery and symbols. Very possibly, virtual reality will lead to an emphasis on learning via symbols. People comprehend images much more quickly than they can grasp columns of numbers or lines of text. The brain's visual processing power has been described by Larry Smarr, director of the National Center for Supercomputing Applications at the University of Illinois: "The eye-brain system is incredibly advanced. Looking at the world, we absorb the equivalent of a billion bits of information per second, as much as the text in 1,000 copies of a magazine. But our mental 'text computer' is limited by the fact that we can read only about 100 bites—or characters—per second."

The feasibility of teaching large proportions of the population to instantly interpret specific symbols is not that difficult. For example, most people in industrially developed societies automatically interpret traffic lights and recognize that red signifies "stop" and that green light allows cars to "go." Citizens of a cyberspace society could be educated to automatically interpret other symbols, whether these be colors, sounds, etc. And visualization designers will produce images (with accompanying sound) that carry inherent meanings. For example, most persons would intuitively recognize that a depiction of an expanding image signifies "more." Tomorrow's classrooms may well have students learning to "read" visualization data much as they learn to read text in contemporary classrooms.

Conclusion

Virtual reality holds much promise for education. But educators need to become involved now to plan for VR's future development, planning, and use with students. To date, the agenda for virtual reality has been set by the computer science community and by the numerous VR vendors. Yet, education has a tremendous wealth of information and experience to bring to VR curriculum.

In closing, this chapter urges educators to become actively involved in virtual reality's progress.

References and Suggested Readings

Benedikt, M. Cyberspace, VR, and the Principle of Commonality. Presentation at Meckler's "Virtual Reality 90" Conference, San Francisco, 1990.

Bowers, C. A. *The Cultural Dimensions of Educational Computing: Understanding the Non-Neutrality of Technology.* New York: Teachers College Press, 1988.

Emmett, A. Down-to-Earth Practical Applications of Virtual Reality Find Commercial Uses. *Computer Graphics World,* March 1992, 46–53.

Gibson, W. *Neuromancer.* New York: Ace Books, 1984.

Habermas, J. *Toward a Rational Society.* Boston, MA: Beacon Press, 1971.

Henderson, J. Cyberspace Representation of Vietnam War Trauma. *Multimedia Review,* Volume 2, Number 4/Volume 3, Number 1– Winter 1991/Spring 1992, 12–23.

Krueger, M. *Artificial Reality II.* Reading, MA: Addison-Wesley, 1991.

Spring, M. Informating with Virtual Reality. In S. K. Helsel and J. P. Ruth, *Virtual Reality: Theory, Practice, and Promise.* Westport, CT: Meckler, 1991.

Smarr, L. From "The Marvels of Virtual Reality." *Fortune Magazine,* June 1991, 138–150.

Stuart, R. The Implications of Education in Cyberspace. *Multimedia Review,* Volume 2, Number 2, Summer 1991, 2(2), 17–28.

Turkle, S. *The Second Self.* New York: Simon and Schuster, 1984.

Chapter 8

A Comprehensive Approach to Preparing Multimedia Designers: A Faculty Perspective

William D. Milheim

Penn State Great Valley

Introduction

Computers and other forms of multimedia technology are becoming increasingly popular as instructional options for corporate training and public school education in a variety of content areas. However, with this increased use comes a greater need for instructional designers and developers with the appropriate education and experience in multimedia technology. While some professionals in this field learn entirely "on-the-job" with little or no academic training, most practitioners rely heavily on a strong academic preparation coupled with appropriate practical experience to obtain their first professional position or promotion into middle or upper management.

This need for strong, academic preparation has prompted faculty members in multimedia design to develop curricula that cross many disciplines and include a variety of experiential options to complement in-class coursework. The goal of this combination of academic preparation and practical work experience is to provide the potential designer with all the skills required to develop effective, interactive, multimedia instruction.

This article describes the basic components of a multimedia design curriculum, including academic coursework, final project options, and practical experience (see Figure 1). It is hoped that these suggestions will assist faculty members and other educators in developing programs that will effectively prepare multimedia designers for their professional roles. While these comments may serve as a basic guide, each multimedia program must be tailored to the students within a specific program, and must include the significant changes that will occur in the future within educational technology or instructional design.

Conceptual Coursework

Academic coursework in various conceptual areas is very important to the preparation of effective multimedia designers and developers, since it provides students with a foundation in understanding how people learn, how to effectively teach, and the methods for appropriately using the technology that multimedia hardware can provide. Specifically, this coursework often includes courses in instructional design, various areas of communication, and innovation/change.

Figure 1

Multimedia Design Curriculum

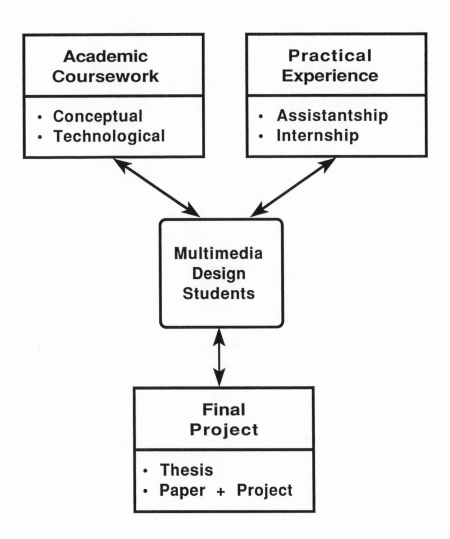

Instructional design coursework should cover all aspects of the design process including a strong emphasis on various instructional design models, such as Gagné, Briggs, and Wager (1992) or Dick and Carey (1990). Additional information concerning appropriate design strategies should also be included, using sources such as Gagné (1987) or Reigeluth (1983, 1987), to provide students with other perspectives of the instructional design process and its accompanying procedures. While these courses may prove to be somewhat repetitive for students with teaching or training backgrounds, they can be quite helpful for students who have no real experience in instructional settings.

Other coursework in this area could include topics such as learning theory, educational statistics, instructional theory, and other relevant areas of educational psychology, with appropriate general texts including, for example, Woolfolk (1987) or Biehler and Snowman (1986). While a variety of these courses may be available within the overall university, care must be taken to adjust a specific course to fit the educational needs of the enrolled multimedia design students.

Communications courses will provide the prospective multimedia developer with skills that may be helpful for working with individuals or within specific organizations. Courses in this area will provide students with strategies for dealing with subject matter experts, working in a team environment, understanding a corporate or educational culture, or designing effective presentations. Specific courses may include human resource development, corporate communications, and interpersonal communications, among others. Courses in these areas are particularly relevant for students intending to work in corporate training environments, where such skills are extremely important.

The final conceptual area important to the academic development of multimedia designers is the study of innovation and change over time, especially as it relates to the use of instructional technology in both education and the corporate sector. Courses such as these focus on effective change models that can be used in various settings and may include specific models for implementing technological change. There are a number of excellent texts in these areas (e.g., Cummings and Huse, 1989; Fullan, 1982; Rogers, 1983), with specific courses often having titles such as "Innovation and Change" or "Organization Development."

Technology-Related Coursework

Another area of significant coursework for students enrolled in multimedia design and development programs typically involves technology-based courses covering various aspects of hardware and software usage. While the specific technology used in these courses will be based on the hardware platforms in use within an academic department, specific coursework should include topics such as basic hardware and software utilization; the design, development, and evaluation of multimedia instructional materials; and present and future uses of multimedia technology.

Basic computer coursework should include detailed information concerning hardware components and software utilization to provide the potential developer with a general understanding of instructional technology and its educational potential. The hardware portion of these courses should include information concerning the functioning of various components, overall hardware integration, and a basic understanding of computer history and technological change over time. Software issues should include, at a minimum, information concerning word processing, databases, spreadsheets, presentation software, and an introduction to the development of computer-based or interactive video instruction.

A second area of technology-related courses should cover the design and development of various types of computer-based instruction. One group of courses in this area could focus on authoring systems and appropriate design strategies that can be used in the development of multimedia instruction. Other courses could concentrate on the application of instructional software in various settings or evaluation strategies for the potential developer or multimedia user. In each of these areas, student coursework should include an emphasis on student projects and the application of various concepts, rather than lengthy written assignments based on academic research. Texts which may be appropriate for these technology-related courses include Alessi and Trollip (1985), Hannafin and Peck (1988), or Jonassen (1988).

The final group of technology-based courses for potential multimedia designers should include a solid preparation in multimedia systems as a whole, including topics such as interactive video, CD-ROM, CD-I, DVI, as well as other forms of multimedia that may be used within education or the corporate sector. Since a variety of media types may be included in a multimedia presentation, this group of courses can also appropriately include information concerning traditional media (videotape, slide-tape, etc.), using a text such as Kemp and Smellie (1989). Potential future developments in the overall field are also relevant in this type of course, since multimedia designers must be on the "cutting edge" of new technologies as well as up-to-date with innovative ideas concerning instructional design, authoring systems, etc.

Final Academic Project

While academic coursework is obviously important for preparing multimedia designers, a final project allows the student to "put it all together" in a single, focused project that draws upon all the significant coursework within a student's academic program. This type of project also allows the faculty within an academic program to effectively judge students concerning their future abilities in multimedia development or other technology-based fields.

Depending on the specific academic program, this final project may take one of two different forms—either a graduate thesis or a final project/paper. The first of these, the thesis, tends to be a research-based project, answering specific questions concerning teaching or learning, such as "What is the most effective ratio of computer information to video scenes in an interactive video lesson?"

The project/paper option often has great diversity in the type of project chosen by a particular student. Potential topics for this option may include, for example, a paper investigating learner control options in computer-based instruction, a project developing an interactive video module covering remedial reading, or other similar ideas. With any of these options, however, the faculty members in an academic program should assist students in obtaining a project that effectively demonstrates the concepts and skills that have been obtained during various courses, while matching, as closely as possible, the specific needs of the individual student.

Practical Experience

While the use of a final academic project allows students to synthesize a significant portion of their coursework, it permits only limited experience in the actual application of course concepts and skills. While this type of project may be very helpful, it may also be beneficial to allow interested students a chance to perform their newly learned skills in a work environment during their program while they are learning in the classroom.

One effective method for providing this experience is through on-campus graduate assistantships, where students become university employees during their graduate coursework. In many subject areas, this assistantship becomes an opportunity for students to do research or teach undergraduate courses in order to gain professional experience or a better knowledge of the subject matter in a particular course.

Such options may be available within multimedia programs, students may be better served with opportunities working as instructional designers or developers in various service organizations within the university (e.g., media services departments or computer-based training centers). This type of experience, while less "academic" in nature, allows students to better understand the specific tasks required of instructional designers in the workplace, and provides potential designers with the opportunity to practice many of the skills and concepts learned previously during their coursework.

While the option for a graduate assistantship is primarily open only to full-time students, the same type of experience is often possible for part-time students through internship experiences in corporate or academic settings. These internships can be full- or part-time and can be tailored specifically to each student's needs by the internship coordinator working with a supervisor at the student's location. Possible settings for this type of experience for multimedia students include training departments in corporate organizations, multimedia development companies, public schools, or various departments within colleges or universities.

Conclusion

The preparation of multimedia designers and developers can be a complicated task consisting of academic preparation in various conceptual areas (instructional design, communications, and innovation/change) as well as technology-related coursework in basic hardware and software, the development and evaluation of multimedia instruction, and coursework in multimedia systems and their individual media components. The last course often presented within these programs is a final project or thesis, which allows students to utilize much of the significant information they have obtained during their academic coursework.

An additional option for some students is employment as a graduate assistant for research, teaching, or design/ development in an area that complements their academic coursework in multimedia design, at a location either within their graduate program or in a service organization elsewhere on campus. Graduate internships (either full- or part-time) are another possibility for gaining additional experience outside the traditional, academic classroom.

While these suggestions may add greatly to the experience of a student in a multimedia design program, it is also important to tailor each course of study to a student's specific goals and objectives within the overall requirements of an academic program. In this sense, an academic program should combine various curricular requirements (coursework, internships, etc.) with the needs of an individual student in order to provide the best possible preparation for a career in multimedia design and development.

References and Suggested Readings

Alessi, S. M., and Trollip, S. R. *Computer-Based Instruction: Methods and Development.* Englewood Cliffs, NJ: Prentice-Hall, 1985.

Biehler, R. F., and Snowman, J. *Psychology Applied to Teaching.* Boston: Houghton Mifflin, 1986.

Cummings, T. G., and Huse, E. F. *Organization Development and Change.* St. Paul, MN: West Publishing, 1989.

Dick, W., and Carey, L. *The Systematic Design of Instruction.* New York: HarperCollins Publishers, 1990.

Fullan, M. *The Meaning of Educational Change.* New York: Teachers College Press, Columbia University, 1982.

Gagné, R. M. (Ed.) *Instructional Technology: Foundations.* Hillsdale, NJ: Lawrence Erlbaum Associates, 1987.

Gagné, R. M., Briggs, L. J., and Wager, W. W. *Principles of Instructional Design.* New York: Harcourt Brace Jovanovich College Publishers, 1992.

Hannafin, M. J., and Peck, K. L. *The Design, Development, and Evaluation of Instructional Software.* New York: Macmillan Publishing, 1988.

Jonassen, D. H. (Ed.) *Instructional Designs for Microcomputer Courseware.* Hillsdale, NJ: Lawrence Erlbaum Associates, 1988.

Kemp, J. E., and Smellie, D. C. *Planning, Producing, and Using Instructional Media.* New York: Harper & Row, 1989.

Reigeluth, C. M. (Ed.) *Instructional-Design Theories and Models: An Overview of Their Current Status.* Hillsdale, NJ: Lawrence Erlbaum Associates, 1983.

Reigeluth, C. M. (Ed.) *Instructional Theories in Action: Lessons Illustrating Selected Theories and Models.* Hillsdale, NJ: Lawrence Erlbaum Associates, 1987.

Rogers, E. M. *Diffusion of Innovations.* New York: The Free Press, 1983.

Woolfolk, A. E. *Educational Psychology.* Englewood Cliffs, NJ: Prentice-Hall, 1987.

Chapter 9

Evaluating Interactive Multimedia

Thomas C. Reeves

University of Georgia

Marcia Linn's 1992 review of the book *Cognition, Education, and Multimedia: Exploring Ideas in High Technology* (Nix and Spiro, 1990), concluded that the extant research suggests that interactive multimedia (IMM) "can help, confuse, or challenge students." The mixed outcomes thus far revealed for this much heralded technology indicate the importance of sound strategies for evaluating it. However, two important questions must be answered before specific methods of evaluating IMM can be presented. What do you mean by IMM? And why are you using IMM?

What Do You Mean
by Interactive Multimedia?

Serious reading of the IMM literature and/or attendance at any of the ever-proliferating IMM conferences leads to the conclusion that some confusion exists about the meaning of this technology (cf., Gygi, 1990). For purposes of this article, IMM is defined as a computerized database that allows users to access information in multiple forms, including text, graphics, video, and audio. IMM is specifically designed with linked nodes of information to allow users to access the information according to their unique needs and interests. (IMM and hypermedia are used synonymously in this article. For more clarification on the distinctions between IMM and hypermedia, or lack thereof, see Reeves and Harmon, 1991.)

The effectiveness of IMM is constrained by two important factors: first, the design of the user interface, and second, the motivation and expertise possessed by the users. Fischer and Mandl (1990), in attempting to develop what they call a "psychophysics" of multimedia, clarify the issue. They maintain that multimedia programs only come into existence when learners perceive and interpret them. The quality of interaction is determined by the skills and experience learners have with the medium *and* the degree to which the medium has been designed to support the interaction.

The two-way nature of the interaction that must exist before IMM comes to existence can be further clarified by a simple analogy. In the same way that an academic library that is void of intelligent faculty and students capable of utilizing its resources is merely a warehouse, multimedia without the interpretative acts of learners is only a collection of textual, graphical, and audio elements. Further, a library in which books and other media are piled in bins at random, with no cataloging system, is useless for even the most dedicated of scholars. Similarly, a multimedia program without a supportive user interface has little value.

The implications of these factors for evaluation are clear. First, it would be difficult and probably futile to evaluate IMM outside the context of its use. Second, individual differences among users with respect to aptitude, knowledge, skills, attitudes, personality characteristics, previous experience, motivation, etc., must be accounted for in any evaluation. Third, the interactions among these individual differences and aspects of the user interface should be a major focus for evaluation.

Why Are You Using Interactive Multimedia?

The second question, that of why are you using IMM, is even more important than the definitional one. In this chapter, the goal of using IMM is assumed to be instruction. (Of course, IMM can serve other purposes, e.g., reference or entertainment, but the evaluation guidelines presented herein assume an instructional focus.) Ideally, the goals of using IMM should be nothing less than fundamentally improving the conditions of teaching and learning in education and training. Corporate leaders in the IMM field have clearly stated their aspirations for this technology. For example, John Sculley, Chief Executive Officer of Apple Computer, Inc., in the Foreword to a book titled *Interactive Multimedia* (Ambron and Hooper, 1988) said:

Teachers and students will command a rich learning [multimedia] environment that, had you described it to me when I was in school, would have seemed entirely magical. Imagine a classroom with a window on all the world's knowledge. Imagine a teacher with the capability to bring to life any image, any sound, any event. Imagine a student with the power to visit any place on earth at any time in history. Imagine a screen that can display in vivid color the inner workings of a cell, the births and deaths of stars, the clashes of armies, and the triumphs of art. And then imagine that you have access to all of this and more by exerting little more effort than simply asking that it appear. It seems like magic even today. Yet the ability to provide this kind of learning environment is within our grasp. (Sculley, 1988, p. *vii*)

James E. Dezell, Jr., formerly Vice-President for Educational Systems at the IBM Corporation and now President of EduQuest, the new IBM Educational Systems Company, is no less an enthusiastic promoter of IMM:

> Multimedia brings to bear dynamic visual information in the form of full-motion video that gives you a direct pipeline into the brain. We, as human beings, process that data very efficiently. The power of full-motion video combined with interactivity allows every person to discover knowledge in the pattern that fits their paradigm for learning—the way they learn best, individualized. (Taylor, 1990, p. 27)

Similar promises are being made in the training world. Steve Roden, President of Comsell, Inc., a training development firm in Atlanta, Georgia, sums it up:

> With multimedia, the policeman is exposed to crisis situations in a less threatening way, the teller understands complicated bank procedures more rapidly, and the PC user can begin to work with a software program faster. There is an enormous validation to this technology's effectiveness in a training environment. Multimedia provides a higher level of mastery over the subject matter. It gives students "hands-on" learning, better retention, specific feedback, and increased levels of understanding. We can't consistently make these statements about videotape, text, text with graphics, traditional classroom learning, or even computer-based training. (Roden, 1991, pp. 80–81)

Although these claims that IMM will provide instructors and students with learning environments of unparalleled richness may seem to border on hyperbole, there would be little point in investing substantial time and resources in this new technology without high aims. Unfortunately, there is a problem with these statements because they seem to imply that IMM *automatically* guarantees learning. The question of whether any specific example of interactive multimedia supports, much less guarantees, learning must be examined carefully. That is precisely the role of evaluation.

Evaluation Perspective

Before specifying guidelines and strategies for the evaluation of IMM, it is important to clarify the perspective or theoretical conception of evaluation on which the guidelines are based. Contemporary perspectives of evaluation range from absolute "measurement" to a completely relativistic "constructivist" perspective (Shadish, Cook, and Leviton, 1991). The former is characterized by the motto "If anything exists, it can be measured." Advocates of the measurement perspective believe that there is an objective reality existing apart from the beliefs of those who seek to reveal it. Measurement proponents seek more precise instruments (e.g., tests) to assess the nature of that ultimate reality (Thorndike, 1982). Their search for finer and finer measures is based on the belief that it is only human weakness that blocks perception of the unchanging natural laws that govern all phenomena, including the processes of human learning. Proponents of national and international achievement tests lean toward this end of the evaluation continuum.

In sharp contrast, the constructivist perspective is characterized by the words of Guba and Lincoln (1989), who wrote: "it [constructivist evaluation] takes the position that evaluation outcomes are not descriptions of the 'way things really are' or 'really work,' or some 'true state of affairs,' but instead represent meaningful constructions that individual actors or groups of actors form to 'make sense' of the situations in which they find themselves" (p. 8). Constructivists generally view measurement as a futile act because the act of measuring always affects what is being measured. Constructivists seek more effective ways of sharing understandings of the world, but ultimately despair of the prediction and control so integral to the measurement perspective. Guba and Lincoln (1989) go so far as to maintain that "To accept the basic premises undergirding responsive constructivist evaluation is virtually to abandon hope that solutions to social problems can ever be found" (p. 47).

Few people would locate themselves at either end of these two extremes of evaluation theory. Instead, while they are likely aware of the limits of measurement in areas as complex as human learning, they view evaluation as an illuminating activity that can assist in solving practical problems. Their ideas about evaluating IMM (or any other phenomena in education and training) are grounded in a pragmatic philosophy.

My own perspective is pragmatic, exemplified by the motto, "Use whatever works to improve the decisions people make." Educational change inevitably involves fallible human beings making decisions. In the absence of reliable, valid information, people still make decisions, relying instead on habit, intuition, prejudice, guessing, or politics. The purpose of evaluation is to provide a more rational basis for decision-making than would otherwise exist.

Formative Evaluation

Evaluation can serve a variety of different roles or functions, including analyzing needs, refining goals and objectives, documenting activities, improving programs and products, assessing effectiveness and impact, and estimating cost effectiveness. It would take many, many pages to describe evaluation guidelines and strategies for each of these roles. However, given the nascent nature of IMM, the emphasis in this article is on *formative evaluation*.

Formative evaluation is "the systematic collection of information for the purpose of informing decisions to design and improve the product" (Flagg, 1990, pp. 1–2). Formative evaluation includes many well-established strategies, such as expert review, observation of individual learners, pilot studies, and field tests. Specific guidelines for these strategies can be found in Flagg's (1990) excellent book, *Formative Evaluation for Educational Technologies*.

In the context of IMM, many of the aforementioned formative evaluation strategies are routinely employed if the IMM is developed through a systematic instructional design (ID) process from initial conceptualization through various "beta" versions of the program. The rest of this article focuses on applying what Newman (1990) defined as "formative experimentation" to IMM programs that have been designated as ready for field implementation, regardless of whether or not they have been developed using a systematic ID process.

Formative Experimentation

It is common practice in the commercial software arena to release programs that have not been completely validated because programs are expected to be "debugged" by the clients who buy version 1.0 of a program. Although at first this may seem unethical, the demands of the marketplace are such that many end-users would rather have innovative software that still has bugs than to wait until the software is flawless. This "real world" situation supports carrying out "formative experimentation" as a formative evaluation strategy for IMM. Newman (1990) describes formative experimentation as follows:

> In a formative experiment, the researcher sets a pedagogical goal and finds out what it takes in terms of materials, organization, or changes in the technology to reach the goal. Instead of rigidly controlling the treatments and observing differences in the outcome, as in a conventional experiment, formative experiments

aim at a particular outcome and observe the process by which the goal is achieved. (p. 10)

According to Newman (1990), "tinkering and careful observation" (p. 12) are hallmarks of the formative experiment. Not surprisingly, many evaluators will resist what appears to be a "trial and error" approach to evaluation. After all, evaluation design as traditionally taught involves experimental or quasi-experimental designs wherein the effects of an instructional innovation (e.g., IMM) are compared with those of "traditional" instruction or some other competing innovation (e.g., computer-based training). This type of "horse race" evaluation is frequently conducted in education and training contexts, with little benefit, due to weaknesses in the comparative evaluation design itself and/or a lack of understanding of the dimensions that are common to both programs (Clark, 1989; Reeves, 1990). In my opinion, evaluations of IMM utilizing experimental or quasi-experimental designs should not be carried out until the IMM is optimized through various formative evaluation strategies, including formative experimentation.

As noted in Newman's (1990) description, a critical component of formative experimentation is the selection of the goals or outcomes that one wishes the technology to achieve. What should be the goals of using IMM for instruction? These goals should be focused on "actualizing" what Resnick (1989) identified as the three primary principles of contemporary cognitive learning theory. First, IMM should be designed to support the principle that learning is a process of knowledge construction as opposed to knowledge absorption. Second, IMM should support the principle that learning is knowledge-dependent, i.e., that people use existing knowledge upon which to build new knowledge. And, third, IMM should support the principle that learning is highly tuned to the situation in which it takes place.

Knowledge Construction and IMM

In traditional instruction, knowledge is taught as an end in itself as opposed to a means to more important ends, such as solving problems (Bransford, Sherwood, Hasselbring, Kinzer, and Williams, 1990). For example, in mathematics, many students struggle to "learn" logarithms, geometric forms, and statistics without perceiving their utility in fields as diverse as astronomy, architecture, and agriculture. In short, content is treated as isolated facts and discrete skills to be "learned" rather than as knowledge, skills, and attitudes to be "used." This is a common error in both education and training contexts.

IMM can be designed to present a focal event or problem situation that serves as an "anchor" or focus for learners' efforts to retrieve and construct knowledge. The knowledge construction process in turn helps learners to understand the event or resolve the problem. Cognitive psychologists call this type of instruction "situated learning" (Collins, Brown, and Newman, 1989) or "anchored instruction" (Bransford *et al.*, 1990) because the process of constructing new knowledge is situated or anchored in meaningful and relevant contexts. In response to these types of events and problems, learners develop (i.e., construct) *useful* as opposed to *inert* knowledge.

Knowledge-Dependent Learning and IMM

According to Glaser (1984) and other cognitive psychologists, knowledge begets knowledge. In other words, the ability to construct new knowledge is a function of both the amount and quality of existing knowledge one has as well as one's reasoning and other intellectual abilities. Because learning depends heavily on what students or trainees already know, IMM should be designed to provide "cognitive bootstrapping" for the construction of knowledge and the development of intellectual skills (Resnick, 1989).

Methods of "bootstrapping" include allowing students to resolve discrepant events, providing them with multiple perspectives of phenomena, and aiding them with perceptual discrimination of complex processes. For example, one way to support the development of new knowledge is to enable students to confront misconceptions they have about various ideas. The construction of new knowledge may be constrained by everyday conceptions of phenomena that conflict with accepted theories (Johsua and Dupin, 1987). Exposing learners to discrepant events permits them to confront their everyday conceptions of the phenomena involved. IMM can be designed to assist learners in resolving discrepancies and ultimately constructing new knowledge on the reconfigured foundations of what they previously "knew."

Situated-Learning and IMM

A major concern for education and training is the degree to which learning transfers to external situations in which the application of knowledge, skills, and attitudes is appropriate. The cognitive theories of Newell and Simon (1972), Anderson (1983), Brown (1985), and others support the fundamental principle that the way in which knowledge, skills, and attitudes are initially learned plays an important role in the degree to which these abilities can be used in other contexts. To put it simply, if knowledge is learned in a context of use, it will be used in that and similar contexts.

In traditional instruction, information is presented in encapsulated formats, and it is largely left up to the student to generate any possible connections between conditions (such as a problem) and actions (such as the use of knowledge as a tool to solve the problem). There is ample evidence that students who are quite adept at "regurgitating" memorized information rarely retrieve that same information when confronted with novel conditions that warrant its application (Bransford *et al.*, 1990). IMM can employ a case-based approach wherein learners are first presented with realistic cases rich with problems to be solved; and then conceptual knowledge, skills, and even attitudes are introduced as required by the individual cases. This enables learners to link newly acquired knowledge in the form of active responses to simulated problems.

An important perspective on how the IMM can transform the conditions for teaching and learning through "situated-learning" is provided by the research of John Seely Brown and his colleagues at Xerox PARC. Collins *et al.* (1989) propose a "cognitive apprenticeship" model of instruction as an effective alternative to traditional instruction. The researchers maintain that traditional instruction abstracts knowledge and skills from their uses in the world. In apprenticeship learning, on the other hand, knowledge and skills are seen as instrumental to the accomplishment of meaningful tasks. The apprenticeship model is based on modeling, coaching, scaffolding, articulating, reflecting, and exploring as opposed to didactic teaching strategies such as telling and correcting. A major benefit of well-designed IMM is that it can include opportunities for simulated apprenticeships as well as a wealth of learning support activities such as modeling and coaching.

Methods of Formative Experimentation

The primary methods to be used in formative experiments are ethnographic ones such as interviews, observations, and records analysis. The unit of analysis for a formative experiment is the school or training center in which the IMM is implemented. A formative experiment should take place in a real setting with meaningful instructional goals. The experiment must be of sufficient duration to allow the IMM to be integrated into the larger instructional milieu or environment. One of the most difficult challenges that evaluators will face is allowing the IMM itself, its implementation, and the very goals at which it is aimed to change over the time of the experiment "as the environment appropriates the technology" (Newman, 1990, p. 12).

How might such an experiment be carried out? Consider a corporate training context, such as sales training for a retail store chain with a high employee turnover. The retail chain has implemented IMM to train new employees and refresh the existing sales force about the chain's sales strategies. The IMM program is "anchored" in a set of typical sales problems that provide opportunities to illustrate how each employee's sales strategies interact and shape the overall success of the company. The IMM system allows trainees to switch perspectives within each simulated problem from that of the sales person to that of the customer, the manager, or a bystander.

The IMM also allows the trainee to consult at any time with a sales "mentor" who provides expert advice on how to handle problems and maximize the potential of various opportunities presented in the program. The electronic mentor provides detailed coaching and modeling as needed or requested.

The evaluator should establish a number of unobtrusive monitoring procedures before the experiment begins. First, the IMM should include automated response-capture routines so that trainee paths and progress through the IMM options are tracked. Second, measures of those individual differences thought to be relevant to the interpretation of outcomes should be incorporated into the IMM. Typically, these will include a questionnaire about certain background variables such as schooling, previous sales experience, and motivation, as well as measures of personality traits such as locus of control. Third, measures of performance should be integrated into the IMM, perhaps using case simulations or *before* and *after* observations of sales performance on the sales floor.

The evaluator should also carefully assess the environment in which the IMM is used by trainees (Reeves, 1991). The evaluator should strive to assure that maximal support is provided for the IMM user with respect to various factors ranging from the quality of the orientation to the system to the comfort of the furniture used with the system, lighting conditions, and audio support.

Unobtrusive observations of learner behavior are also advised in formative experiments, especially if the IMM is designed to be used by two or more learners collaboratively. Capturing the nature of interactions among learners can be especially fruitful in understanding their perceptions of IMM and the type of cognitive processes in which they engage.

Questionnaires and interviews can be used at various points in the experiment to provide information about specific aspects of the IMM and its integration into the training environment. Interviews will generally be preferred over questionnaires because of the flexibility of protocols that permit exploration of unanticipated themes. A major focus of the questionnaires and interviews should be upon learners' understanding and appreciation of the IMM user interface.

Ideally, formative experimentation data should be reviewed on a continual basis to guide improvement of various aspects of the IMM and its implementation. The goal of this feedback and tinkering is maximizing the capacity of the IMM to attain its stated goals. In a sense, a formative experiment is only concluded when the desired goal is achieved without extraordinary external support by the evaluator and IMM developers.

Conclusion

The evaluation activities described in this chapter have the potential to make significant progress toward improving education and training. Robert Ebel, past president of the American Educational Research Association, said that education "is in need of creative invention to make it work better" (Farley, 1982). Contemporary IMM programs such as IBM's *Discover Columbus* (IBM Presents *Columbus* and the *Classics*, 1991) and Apple Computer's *The Encyclopedia of Multimedia* (Doyle, 1989) represent very creative invention. However, even creative invention is inadequate unless it is guided by sound evaluation.

References

Ambron, S., and Hooper, K. (Eds.) *Interactive Multimedia*. Redmond, WA: Microsoft Press, 1988.

Anderson, J. R. *The Architecture of Cognition*. Cambridge, MA: Harvard University Press, 1983.

Bransford, J. D., Sherwood, R. D., Hasselbring, T. S., Kinzer, C. K., and Williams, S. M. Anchored Instruction: Why We Need It and How Technology Can Help. In D. Nix and R. Spiro (Eds.), *Cognition, Education, and Multimedia: Exploring Ideas in High Technology*. Hillsdale, NJ: Lawrence Erlbaum, 1990, 115–141.

Brown, J. S. Process Versus Product: A Perspective on Tools for Communal and Informal Electronic Learning. *Journal of Educational Computing Research*, 1985, 1, 179–201.

Clark, R. E. Current Progress and Future Directions for Research in Instructional Technology. *Educational Technology Research and Development*, 1989, 37(1), 57–66.

Collins, A., Brown, J. S., and Newman, S. E. Cognitive Apprenticeship: Teaching the Crafts of Reading, Writing, and Mathematics. In L. B. Resnick (Ed.), *Knowing, Learning, and Instruction: Essays in Honor of Robert Glaser*. Hillsdale, NJ: Lawrence Erlbaum, 1989, 453–494.

Doyle, D. *The Encyclopedia of Multimedia* [computer program]. Cupertino, CA: Apple Computer, Inc., 1989.

Farley, F. H. The Future of Educational Research. *Educational Researcher*, 1982, *11*(8), 11–19.

Fischer, P. M., and Mandl, H. Introduction: Toward a Psychophysics of Hypermedia. In D. H. Jonassen and H. Mandl (Eds.), *Designing Hypermedia for Learning*. Heidelberg, Germany: Springer-Verlag, 1990.

Flagg, B. N. *Formative Evaluation for Educational Technologies*. Hillsdale, NJ: Lawrence Erlbaum, 1990.

Glaser, R. Education and Thinking: The Role of Knowledge. *American Psychologist*, 1984, *39*, 93–104.

Guba, E. G., and Lincoln, Y. S. *Fourth Generation Evaluation*. Newbury Park, CA: Sage Publications, 1989.

Gygi, K. Recognizing the Symptoms of Hypertext . . . and What to Do About It. In B. Laurel (Ed.), *The Art of Human-Computer Interface Design*. Reading, MA: Addison-Wesley, 1990.

IBM Presents *Columbus* and the *Classics. Multimedia and Videodisc Monitor*, May 1991, *9*(5), 1, 3.

Johsua, S., and Dupin, J. J. Taking into Account Student Misconceptions in Instructional Strategy: An Example in Physics. *Cognition and Instruction*, 1987, *4*, 117–125.

Linn, M. D. The Art of Multimedia and the State of Education. *Educational Researcher*, 1992, *21*(1), 30–32.

Newell, A., and Simon, H. *Human Problem-Solving*. Englewood Cliffs, NJ: Prentice-Hall, 1972.

Newman, D. Opportunities for Research on the Organizational Impact of School Computers. *Educational Researcher*, 1990, *19*(3), 8–13.

Nix, D., and Spiro, R. (Eds.) *Cognition, Education, and Multimedia: Exploring Ideas in High Technology*. Hillsdale, NJ: Lawrence Erlbaum, 1990.

Reeves, T. C. Redirecting Evaluation of Interactive Video: The Case for Complexity. *Studies in Educational Evaluation*, 1990, *16*, 115–131.

Reeves, T. C. Ten Commandments for the Evaluation of Interactive Multimedia in Higher Education. *Journal of Computing in Higher Education*, 1991, *2*, 84–113.

Reeves, T. C., and Harmon, S. W. What's in a Name—Hypermedia Versus Multimedia. *Interact*, 1991, *3*(1), 28–30.

Resnick, L. B. *Knowing, Learning, and Instruction: Essays in Honor of Robert Glaser*. Hillsdale, NJ: Lawrence Erlbaum, 1989.

Roden, S. Multimedia: The Future of Training. *Ultimedia Digest*, 1991, *1*, 78–81.

Sculley, J. Foreword. In S. Ambron and K. Hooper (Eds.), *Interactive Multimedia*. Redmond, WA: Microsoft Press, 1988.

Shadish, W. R., Cook, T. D., and Leviton, L. C. *Foundations of Program Evaluation: Theories of Practice*. Newbury Park, CA: Sage Publications, 1991.

Taylor, B. A. An Agent for Education Change: Interview with Jim Dezell. *Human Capital*, 1990, *1*(2), 24–27.

Thorndike, R. L. *Applied Psychometrics*. Boston, MA: Houghton Mifflin, 1982.

Chapter 10

The Future of Multimedia: Bridging to Virtual Worlds

Christopher J. Dede

George Mason University

In a world where data increases exponentially each year, a major challenge for schools is to prepare students to access and use information effectively. Learners frequently become lost in a morass of data from texts and from inquiry projects. Without higher-order thinking skills, they cannot synthesize large volumes of information into overarching knowledge structures. As rich technologies such as multimedia provide increasing amounts of data in which learners can drown, this shortfall of current educational practice is being repeated across the crowded curriculum.

The same technologies that are swamping students in information can help learners master thinking skills for assimilating this data. This requires a refocusing of current uses of multimedia in the curriculum, from engines for transmitting massive amounts of data to tools for structured inquiry based on higher-order thinking. Such an approach is generic across a range of disciplines, from science and mathematics to social sciences and humanities.

Reconceptualizing multimedia now is important because, over the next decade, the fusion of computers and telecommunications will lead to the development of highly realistic virtual environments that are collaborative and interactive. As discussed later in this article, the evolution of this "meta-medium" will enable artificial realities that immerse students in information-laden virtual worlds. Such learning environments risk overwhelming their users unless they incorporate tools that help students and teachers to master the cognitive skills essential to synthesizing knowledge from data.

Multimedia in schools must bridge from its current role of augmenting data delivery in conventional instruction to instead fostering a new model of teaching/learning based on learners' navigation and creation of knowledge webs. Such a transformation requires evolving today's often fragmentary multimedia applications into more structured inquiry approaches that build on web-like architectures from hypermedia. As a further stage of development, through advances in visualization and virtual communities, multimedia can become the basis for rich virtual "worlds" that provide both intellectual and emotional stimulation.

This chapter briefly describes two stages of multimedia's potential development: incorporating hypermedia to enable knowledge construction by learners, and using visualization and virtual communities to create artificial worlds. Such an evolution would make multimedia the core of an information infrastructure that could be a driveshaft for educational reform. Without such a transformation, multimedia risks continuing its present status as a hood ornament for the conventional classroom, contributing some motivation at the risk of causing intellectual indigestion through information overload.

Multimedia and Hypermedia

Multimedia technologies have great potential to empower learners' mastery of higher-order thinking skills. The leverage that sophisticated multimedia provides stems from a synthesis of multiple attributes rather than any single characteristic: learning via structured discovery; motivational power; ability to tap multiple learning styles; web-like representations of knowledge; enhanced mastery through learner authoring of materials; the collection of rich evaluative information; technology-supported collaborative inquiry. At a time when the educational reform movement is providing momentum for change, the sophisticated multimedia devices that are necessary to support these instructional attributes are finally becoming affordable for schools. The availability of this technological infrastructure enables extending beyond current multimedia implementations to new types of instructional strategies that take advantage of multimedia's unique capabilities.

In June, 1990, our research group at George Mason University's Center for Interactive Educational Technology (CIET) began designing a multimedia prototype to foster higher-order thinking skills (Fontana, 1991). Our ultimate goal is to build a generic instructional shell for thinking skills that can be easily customized to multimedia content across a range of disciplines, from science and mathematics to the social sciences and humanities. As an initial step toward that objective, The Civil War Interactive Project uses Ken Burns' documentary series on PBS, *The Civil War*, as the core of its multimedia database. With short-term funding from the Corporation for Public Broadcasting and George Mason University and with limited technical assistance from Apple

Computer, our team has produced a design demonstration for a computer-based instructional system that teaches a structured process for higher-order thinking while learners engage in guided historical inquiry.

We are now planning a second stage of this research: developing prototype curricula in both history/social science (the Civil War) and science (science literacy) within an instructional shell that illustrates a new paradigm for inquiry-based learning. The prototypes will have four generic, essential features: the IBI (Inquiry Bureau of Investigation), Dr. Know, the Production Console, and Guided Tours. The IBI is literally an iconic bureau; by opening each of its drawers, students will receive instruction on the steps of inquiry. Dr. Know is the context-sensitive coach who helps students develop data-gathering and metacognitive skills; he/she introduces students to the IBI and is readily available to give advice. The Production Console gives students tools with which to manipulate the information in the database and create their own tours. Guided Tours provide exemplary illustrations of using the abstract inquiry skills discussed in the IBI to structure a specific set of data.

Our Thinking Skills Project views students as tourists through multimedia databases. Just as tourists make choices about how they will explore different sights, users of our thinking skills shell can decide how to explore their cognitive environment; they may choose one of several Guided Tours or can explore the database in a free-form manner. A reflective context for learning is created in the exemplary Guided Tours; these provide stimulating environments within which students become actively engaged in learning the subject domain while receiving context-sensitive instruction on the inquiry process. As students proceed through the database, they are able to call up their on-line Journal to take notes; to make copies of documents; and to select photographs, graphics, and segments of video or audio that they will later assess and evaluate as part of their work in the Production Console.

In reviewing a sample of multimedia materials presently available to schools, our design is unique in providing students with an intelligent tool that can be used to develop skills in managing information. In contrast to the jumbles of data many current multimedia products present, our prototypes will:

- deliver explicit instruction in the steps of inquiry in the IBI;
- provide, via the Guided Tours, implicit instruction on the steps of inquiry and on modeling thinking strategies and knowledge structures;
- incorporate a context-sensitive coach (Dr. Know), who helps students use their skills as they encounter the knowledge base;
- position the Production Console as a vital element in both instruction and evaluation, enabling students to create sophisticated products for their portfolios;
- build from video created by talented artists adept at making visual material intellectually and emotionally compelling; and
- include large bodies of primary source materials as the building blocks of the knowledge base.

Hypermedia provides a representational architecture very important in actualizing these capabilities in a multimedia database.

Hypermedia—the associative, nonlinear interconnection of multimedia materials—extends conventional multimedia in several ways (Dede and Palumbo, 1991):

- The associative, nonlinear nature of hypermedia mirrors the structure of human long-term memory, lessening users' need to map from how computers represent data to how people store information.

- The capability of hypermedia to reveal and conceal the complexity of its content lessens the cognitive load on users of this medium, thereby enhancing their ability to assimilate and manipulate ideas.
- The structure of hypermedia facilitates capturing and communicating knowledge, as opposed to fragmented data, allowing users to view their own mental models as visual webs of nodes/links.
- Hypermedia's architecture enables distributed, coordinated interaction, a vital component of teamwork, organizational memory, and other "group mind" phenomena.

Multimedia systems that store the pattern of users' traversal through the database, such as our projected thinking skills shell, enable learners, teachers, and researchers to track students' progression through knowledge webs in the content material. This allows more reflective learning, as well as sophisticated evaluation strategies that trace shifts in students' patterns of thought.

To achieve this vision, the concept of hypermedia must shift from its current focus on knowledge presentation (i.e., an easy authoring system) to sophisticated knowledge representation and finally toward knowledge construction (Nelson and Palumbo, in press). Instructional design issues for knowledge representation using web structures include:

- How many levels of subnetworks can be supported before users become disoriented traversing the structure (the "lost in hyperspace" problem)?

- How rich can the branching structure be at nodes before the cognitive overhead required for user choices outweighs the value of nonlinear representation?
- How can the knowledge in a database be equably distributed among nodes (which convey data) and links (which convey relationships)?
- For collaborative learning, how can situations be avoided in which users become confused about how a colleague has altered the knowledge web (the "Tower of Babel" problem)?

As multimedia instructional systems evolve to explicit use of hypermedia architectures, these types of design issues will become increasingly important.

The ultimate potential of hypermedia is to evolve beyond knowledge representation to knowledge construction, so that the learner can modify/add nodes and links. Few hypermedia systems provide tools to support this type of activity, yet these capabilities are crucial to advance students past passively assimilating knowledge to actively creating their own mental models. Research and development in this area, as illustrated in our thinking skills shell by the Production Console, are essential to shifting multimedia from a visual database to a knowledge construction set. Such an evolution is crucial to the development of evaluation systems that move beyond measuring factual retention into assessing mastery of higher-order cognitive skills.

In Schrage (1990), Alan Kay analyzes the implications of new media through the question, "What does a medium ask you to become in order to use it?" Print requires a rational reader; television, a passive observer; the telephone, a conversationalist. When structured into learning environments that motivate guided inquiry, hypermedia has the potential to develop more user metacognition (thinking about thinking) than linear media.

While reading, listening, and viewing are passive in linear media, web structures demand continuous choice and navigation on the part of the learner. This strength of hypermedia representations provides a bridge for transforming fragmentary multimedia databases into richly detailed virtual worlds.

Virtual Worlds

Instructional applications are gradually shifting away from tutorials, simulations, games, and drill-and-practice into multimedia/hypermedia environments designed to motivate and guide student exploration. Richly detailed multimedia "worlds" that mimic, but simplify and extend the real world, leverage three variables that enhance learning. First, multimedia can reach a broader range of student learning styles than any single medium. Second, learning situated in virtual worlds similar to the real-world setting in which knowledge and skills will be applied is more likely to transfer (The Cognition and Technology Group at Vanderbilt, 1990). Third, multimedia worlds can be strongly motivating if their designers incorporate elements that stimulate fantasy, challenge, and curiosity to increase emotional involvement (Malone and Lepper, 1985).

Beyond these levers for enhancing students' mastery of material, multimedia has the potential to support two types of "magic" strongly conducive to learning: visualization and virtual communities. Simulations that merely mimic reality have their uses, such as allowing learners to experience activities that are dangerous or expensive. However, adding the ability to magically act in ways impossible in the real world opens up new dimensions for instruction, as well as opportunities for fantasy and curiosity. Through visualization, learners can manipulate typically intangible entities such as molecules and mental models; through virtual communities, students can interact in rich psychosocial environments populated by simulated beings.

Visualization

Imagine a student interested in medicine entering a multimedia-based virtual room labeled "Laboratory." Inside are three types of objects with which to interact. First, the learner can explore the uses of commonplace laboratory devices such as microscopes and centrifuges. Second, the learner can manipulate typically intangible physical objects such as molecules, altering their size to perceive three-dimensional configuration and maneuvering two molecules together to understand how one catalyzes a change in the other. Third, the learner can perform similar actions with typically intangible cognitive objects, such as mental models or knowledge structures, looking for patterns that expose the similarities and differences of contrasting theories.

Such a virtual medical laboratory would support two types of visualization: "sensory transducers" that allow users' eyes, ears, and hands to access previously imperceptible phenomena (such as a molecule), and "cognitive transducers" that perform a similar function for intellectual entities. Sensory transducers provide a means of grasping reality through illusion (Brooks, 1988). Using computers to expand human perceptions (e.g., allowing a medical student—like Superman—to see the human body through X-ray vision) is a powerful method for deepening learners' intuitions about physical phenomena.

Cognitive transducers, a second form of visualization, make intellectual entities such as knowledge structures visible and manipulable. They are a logical extension of sensory transducers in enhancing the power of virtual learning environments. Transforming the symbolic into the geometric via data visualization is useful in situations where the amount of data is large, and interacting with the data to shape its presentation can aid in interpretation.

A leading-edge illustration of generic data visualization approaches is the Information Visualizer, an experimental interface that uses color and three-dimensional, interactive animation to create information objects (Robertson, Card, and Mackinlay, 1991). Designers of educational "microworlds" (simulations in which the user can change the rules by which the virtual environment functions) also frequently incorporate cognitive transducers. For example, the Alternate Reality Kit allows the user to see and manipulate iconic representations of abstractions such as Newton's Law of Gravity (Smith, 1987).

As one example of applying cognitive transducers in education, the author has conducted preliminary research on the functional design of an information tool to aid instructional developers (Dede and Jayaram, 1990). By allowing the user to traverse virtual cognitive space, such an application could image the mental models that underlie training. The viewer could navigate through a virtual environment populated by cognitive entities represented as physical objects. In addition, the user could transcend the metaphor of physical space by shifting among alternate contexts (e.g., informational, relational, diagnostic) that provide different perspectives on a particular cognitive entity. Special capabilities to minimize complexity (i.e., guided tours, filters) would also be available.

Multimedia/hypermedia is a powerful representational architecture to support these types of visualization; computer graphics and video can be combined to create a richly detailed, magical virtual world, in which interconnections among data can be made visually explicit. As multimedia environments that support visualization become more common, instructional designers will face new types of challenges. Just as current instructional systems must match a mixture of textual, auditory, visual, and psychomotor presentations to the student's learning style, so virtual worlds that use visualization must balance representations of physical objects, sensory transducers, and cognitive transducers. Developing rhetorics for transducing typically intangible physical and intellectual entities is also a major challenge.

Visualization is one form of magic that empowers learning in multimedia environments; a second type of magic is virtual communities. Learners can interact in psychosocial environments populated both by video-links to other people and by simulated beings. These simulated beings may be avatars (computer graphics representations of people) or knowbots (machine-based agents); each adds an important dimension to education in virtual worlds.

Virtual Communities, Knowbots, and Avatars

As discussed earlier, situating training in virtual contexts similar to the environments in which learners' skills will be used helps their knowledge to transfer. When the material involved has psychosocial as well as intellectual dimensions, the design of authentic experiences to embed in multimedia worlds becomes more complex. In addition to physical and cognitive entities, instructional developers can include simulated beings (avatars and knowbots) in the virtual environment.

One example of such an educational application involves software engineering training (Stevens, 1989). Using hypermedia, Digital Video Interactive (DVI), and rule-based expert systems, the Advanced Learning Technologies Project at Carnegie Mellon University has created a multimedia environment similar to a typical corporate setting. The trainee interacts with this virtual world in the role of a just-hired software engineer still learning the profession. Through direct instruction and simulated experience, the student practices the process of formal code inspection.

The learner can access various rooms in the virtual software company, including an auditorium, library, office, training center, and conference facility. Machine-based agents (knowbots) that simulate people, such as a trainer and a librarian, facilitate the use of resources to learn about the code inspection process. Via specialized tools in the office, the student can prepare for a simulated code inspection, in which he or she can choose to play any of three roles out of the four roles possible in this formal software review process. For each inspection, a rule-based expert system utilizes DVI technology to construct knowbots that simulate the three roles not chosen by the learner. This knowledge-based system controls the topic of conversation; determines who should speak next; and models the personalities of the knowbots in the inspection meeting, altering their cognitive and affective perspective depending on what is happening.

The learner uses a menu-based natural language interface to interact with these simulated beings, who model behaviors typical in code inspection situations. The student not only can choose from a wide range of options of what to say, but also can determine when to make remarks, and can select the emotional inflection of his or her utterances, from a calm, passive tone to an angry, aggressive snarl. By mimicking the reactions likely from human participants in a real simulation, the knowbots provide the learner with a sense of the strengths and weaknesses of different intellectual/psychosocial strategies for that role in a code inspection.

Without using multimedia worlds and knowbots, this type of authentic experience is very difficult to simulate in classroom settings. Not only is the instructional environment dissimilar from the corporate context in which software development skills will be used, but also students do not know how to roleplay exemplary, typical, and problematic participants in code inspections. Through knowbots, the instructional designer can provide paradigmatic illustrations of how to handle a variety of situations, without the expense of having teams of human actors perform for each individual learner.

The simulated beings in virtual learning environments need not all be machine-based agents. Telepresence allows people to interact across distance via avatars (computer-graphics representations of remotely located human agents), as well as direct video-links. For example, SIMNET (Orlansky and Thorp, 1991) is a training application that creates a virtual battlefield on which learners at remote sites can simultaneously operate military equipment. Complex data-objects that indicate changes in the state of each piece of equipment are exchanged via a telephone network interconnecting the training workstations ("dial-a-war"). The appearance and capabilities of graphics-based avatars representing military personnel alter second-by-second as the virtual battle evolves. Through this telepresence approach, a widely distributed group of personnel can engage in simulated real-time warfare without the necessity of gathering the participants at a single site to conduct combat. Telecommunications capabilities that can enable widely distributed, high-bandwidth multimedia environments for a much broader range of sophisticated educational uses will soon be affordable by schools (Dede, 1991; Pea and Gomez, in press).

Participants in a virtual world interacting via avatars tend to treat each other as imaginary beings. An intriguing example of this phenomenon is documented in research on Lucasfilm's Habitat (Morningstar and Farmer, 1991). Habitat was initially designed to be an on-line entertainment medium in which people could meet in a virtual environment to play adventure games. Users, however, extended the system into a full-fledged virtual community with a unique culture; rather than playing pre-scripted fantasy games, they focused on creating new lifestyles and utopian societies.

As an entertainment-oriented virtual world, Habitat provided participants the opportunity to get married or divorced (without real-world repercussions), start businesses (without risking money), found religions (without real-world persecution), murder other's avatars (without moral qualms), and tailor the appearance of one's own avatar to assume a range of personal identities (e.g., movie star, dragon). Just as SIMNET enables virtual battles, Habitat and its successors empower users to create artificial societies. What people want from such societies that the real world cannot offer is magic, such as the gender-alteration machine (Change-o-matic) that was one of the most popular devices in the Habitat world.

In summary, giving users magical powers opens up learning in ways that educators are just beginning to understand. As with any emerging medium, first traditional types of instructional content are being ported to multimedia worlds; eventually, alternative, unique forms of expression—like Habitat—will be created to take advantage of expanded capabilities for communication and learning.

Implications of Emerging Multimedia Worlds

The psychosocial implications of multimedia environments are complex and depend in part on how the interchange between learners and subject matter is structured. However, regardless of the instructional design underlying any specific application, the medium also shapes the message; and the impacts on learners of emerging media such as virtual worlds are still uncertain. The potentially troubling effects of mediating human experience through technology are nowhere more clear than in the community (Dede, 1991). The single greatest experiential input for many Americans now is the pervasive sensory, informational, and normative environment created by television, radio, videogames, movies, and videotapes. In this situation, people's knowledge and values can be constrained by the characteristics of these communications channels.

For example, concerns about "reality pollution" in the news media are mounting. Businesses produce and distribute self-serving, sometimes biased "docutainments" that the media broadcast to cheaply augment their programming. Images can now be doctored electronically to the point that their authenticity can no longer be determined. Political events are routinely followed by commentaries in which "spin control" experts attempt to skew viewers' perspectives on what they saw.

The cultural consequences of technology-mediated physical/social environments are mixed. On the one hand, people have a wider range of vicarious experience and more contact with specialized human resources than they could attain through direct interaction in their local region. On the other hand, to the extent that our perceptions of family life come from situation comedies, of crime from police shows, and of sexuality from soap operas—and to the degree that our physical exercise is confined to pressing the buttons on videogames—this society is in serious trouble.

The technologies themselves do not dictate content that creates a "couch potato" mentality or implies all of life's problems can be solved in thirty minutes. As pervasive interpreters of reality, the American media are influenced primarily by economic, political, and cultural forces. But, given that the medium does intrinsically shape the message, multimedia developers must consider the extent to which non-interactive communications technologies have generated passive, narcotic behavior for many in our society.

Technology evolves in waves of innovation and consolidation. The advent of "motion pictures" about a century ago ushered in civilization's fourth medium, another dimension to communication beyond spoken language, written language, and still images. Later, new technologies appeared to embellish the capabilities of moving images: broadcast and narrowcast television, videotapes, videodiscs, multimedia, hypermedia. Now all of these are merging into a synthesis so far beyond its individual components that it constitutes a new medium: artificial realities.

Part of the educational implications of this medium center around its channel, which is rich and powerful enough to mimic the meta-medium in which we live, the real world. Other instructional implications come from the educational features multimedia worlds can support: sensory and cognitive transducers, virtual communities made up of people's avatars and of machine-based knowbots. The nonlinearity and interactivity of this new medium are exciting in their potential to bridge beyond the limitations of sequential, passive media such as television.

Any powerful information technology is a double-edged sword: a source of either propaganda or education. Through advances in information technology, multimedia environments can now be created that seem intensely real to participants, yet may be false to the true nature of reality in the same way that fractally-generated mountain ranges are not valid depictions of physical topography and geology. Multimedia worlds, virtual communities, and knowbots are emerging technologies that have enormous potential to improve training. However, trainers and learners must recognize that these instructional vehicles carry intrinsic content that can empower or subvert the goals of an educational experience. Careful research is needed to understand how to optimize the design and utilization of multimedia worlds for training.

References

Brooks, Jr., F. P. Grasping Reality Through Illusion: Interactive Graphics Serving Science. *CHI '88 Proceedings.* Reading, MA: Addison-Wesley, 1988, 1–11.

Brown, J. S., Collins, A., and Duguid, P. Situated Cognition and the Culture of Learning. *Educational Researcher*, 1989, *18*(1), 32–42.

The Cognition and Technology Group at Vanderbilt. Anchored Instruction and Its Relationship to Situated Cognition. *Educational Researcher*, 1990, *19*(6), 2–10.

Dede, C. J. Emerging Information Technologies: Implications for Distance Learning. *Annals of the American Academy for Political and Social Sciences*, March 1991, *14*, 146–158.

Dede, C. J., and Jayaram, G. *Designing a Training Tool for Imaging Mental Models* (AFHRL Technical Report CR-90-80). Brooks AFB, TX: Air Force Human Resources Laboratory, 1990.

Dede, C., and Palumbo, D. Implications of Hypermedia for Cognition and Communication. *Impact Assessment Bulletin 9*, 1–2 (Summer, 1991), 15–28.

Fontana, L. A. The Civil War Interactive. *Instruction Delivery Systems*, November/December 1991, *5*(6), 5–9.

Malone, T. W., and Lepper, M. R. Making Learning Fun: A Taxonomy of Intrinsic Motivations for Learning. In R. E. Snow and M. J. Farr (Eds.), *Aptitude, Learning, and Instruction III. Cognitive and Affective Process Analysis.* Hillsdale, NJ: Lawrence Erlbaum, 1985, 176–189.

Morningstar, C., and Farmer, F. R. The Lessons of Lucasfilm's Habitat. In M. Benedikt (Ed.), *Cyberspace: First Steps.* Cambridge, MA: MIT Press, 1991, 273–302.

Nelson, W., and Palumbo, D. Implications for Hypermedia in Education. *Journal of Educational Multimedia and Hypermedia*, in press.

Orlansky, J., and Thorp, J. SIMNET—An Engagement Training System for Tactical Warfare. *Journal of Defense Research*, 1991, *20*(2), 774–783.

Pea, R. D., and Gomez, L. M. Distributed Multimedia Learning Environments: Why and How. *Interactive Learning Environments*, in press.

Robertson, G., Card, S., and Mackinlay, J. The Information Visualizer. *Proceedings of CHI 91.* New York: Association for Computing Machinery, 1991, 181–188.

Schrage, M. *Shared Minds: The New Technologies of Collaboration.* New York: Random House, 1990.

Smith, R. B. Experiences with the Alternate Reality Kit: An Example of the Tension Between Literalism and Magic. *Proceedings of CHI + GI 1987.* New York: Association for Computing Machinery, 1987, 324–333.

Stevens, S. Intelligent Interactive Video Simulation of a Code Inspection. *Communications of the ACM, 32(7),* 1989, 832–843.

Chapter 11

Getting Started in Multimedia: Avoiding Common Pitfalls

Diane M. Gayeski

As we have seen, multimedia holds many possibilities for professionals in education, training, and communications. A big problem is just how to get started: there are so many options for program formats and system configurations. Based on my own experiences and general knowledge of the history of educational technologies, here are some pointers:

Start out simple. Don't feel that you need to use the most sophisticated systems or designs available—especially if you're new to interactive media. Choose hardware and software that will allow you to get up and running quickly so that early efforts can be directed toward solving instructional problems and developing intriguing designs—not fighting with the electronics. Some early successes with simple systems will do a lot to enhance your confidence and motivation, and the opinions of potential sponsors and users.

Budget for R&D. Experimenting with new multimedia systems takes time and money. Often, this can't be done under the constraints of "real" projects and deadlines. Instead, set aside some time, money, and facilities to develop prototypes of actual programs which you may actually produce in the future—or re-makes of programs using other hardware delivery systems. These prototypes allow you to learn new skills and evaluate new systems, and also show potential sponsors and clients your capabilities.

Get the best information. Most designers and developers get the majority of their information about new technologies from hardware vendors—either through ads, trade shows, or sales calls. Although they are certainly one source of information, they are undoubtedly biased and generally uninformed about alternatives other than their own products. Typical magazine articles and conference presentations may be a little better, but few expose the problems that people encounter in multimedia projects. Rather, ask the advice of experienced users who are not trying to sell you either their production services or hardware/software systems. A few books and some modest consultation fees can save you years of headaches and rooms full of incompatible and ineffective systems.

Set the stage first. When introducing multimedia systems, it's often more than just putting out a few new boxes. For many organizations, it means going from traditional classroom-based instruction to self-study. Detailed response files and scores may be maintained for the first time. Instructors become developers. And more attention will be paid to each word and image coming from the multimedia system than would be paid to such data being presented in more traditional ways. Make sure the political and managerial systems are ready for these changes. Determine how new developers will be evaluated, who will control the delivery systems and users' access to them, who is responsible for updating courses, and what will be done with the users' response files. The real shift is moving from *instruction* (measured in terms of pages, hours, or numbers of students) to *performance* (measured by mastery tests or actual work output).

Leverage existing equipment. Many people ask me which platform is best; my typical response is to use whatever is most common within the rest of the organization. If IBM PC-compatibles are used in your offices, work with that platform, even if a Macintosh might be more elegant for your application or an Amiga is cheaper. Likewise, most academic institutions have many Macintoshes in writing and computer labs; if that's your situation, use a Mac. It's important to minimize the differences between multimedia hardware and what's already being used as productivity tools. This builds upon user experience and an installed base of equipment and expertise. It also positions you more in the center of an organization's functioning rather than as some "crazy technologist" with "strange devices."

Buy several inexpensive tools rather than one elaborate one. Novices often get hung up trying to find the one "perfect" authoring tool. By trying to license one that has every possible feature, you generally get one that's very difficult to use and is probably expensive. It's better to buy several simpler tools which excel in creating certain types of applications—such as computer-generated slide shows, tutorials, or hypertext—since no one authoring tool really does *all* of these jobs equally well. I have also seen people spend more money and time on evaluating authoring systems than it would have cost them to merely buy three or four! The most significant expenditure is the time it takes to select, learn, and apply tools—not the tools themselves.

Produce tools, not shows. Unfortunately, multimedia is often seen as expensive toys—entertainment devices in the category of commercial TV or video games. We have to consciously avoid this trap by producing simple but elegant tools which improve performance—most desirably, right within the present user's context of the classroom or workplace. Five simple but powerful job aids or reference tools are much better output than one expensive and dramatic program with limited application requiring dedicated and expensive playback systems.

Spend resources on assessment, not glitz. Often producers will spend a lot of time and money producing fancy special effects or graphics, yet just slap together a few poorly written multiple choice questions for a mastery test. Remember, in multimedia, the users' experience depends upon the way the program handles their responses to questions or options. If embedded items are too easy, no one will ever see the remedial branches; if mastery tests are technically inadequate, the scores will be invalid. This becomes especially important when response files are to be used as evidence of mastery or later used for hiring, promotion, or grading. The legal implications of this are immense. I find it amazing that producers generally don't hesitate to hire a graphic artist for $75/hour to develop dazzling images, but don't have the budget to bring in an expert in testing and assessment! In addition to developing test items, you'll probably be asked to cost-justify multimedia; be prepared to offer data-based evidence.

Plan for reviews and updating. Multimedia will draw a lot of attention—especially at first. This means that the content of the program will draw much more attention than similar material presented in a traditional form by a teacher or trainer. Expect long approval times and lots of critiques. Also, plan for how the material will be updated when it becomes outdated. Consider ease of modification of programs (by non-programmers) when evaluating software tools; many systems allow changes to be made as easily as word-processing; others take a lot of skill and time to change.

The pages that follow (see the Appendix) contain some models and resources you can use to jump-start your multimedia efforts. First, assess your organization's interactive skills using the profile survey. Next, consider the types of systems you should implement using the decision model. Based on that, look over the typical budget to get an idea of what you'll need to purchase. Use the authoring tool checklist as an aid to choosing your software tools. Finally, look over the lists of organizations, periodicals, and books to amplify and update your knowledge of multimedia.

Appendix

Interactive Skills Profile

	Degree of Expertise $\longrightarrow$				
Knowledge of content area	I	I	I	I	I
Experience in explaining content	I	I	I	I	I
Knowledge of end-users	I	I	I	I	I
Instructional design skills	I	I	I	I	I
Knowledge of hardware systems	I	I	I	I	I
Scriptwriting	I	I	I	I	I
Graphic production/layout	I	I	I	I	I
Test construction/validation	I	I	I	I	I
Flowcharting/interactive design	I	I	I	I	I
Ability to use authoring tool(s)	I	I	I	I	I
Video/audio production capability	I	I	I	I	I
Project management skills	I	I	I	I	I
Evaluation/cost assessment skill	I	I	I	I	I

Multimedia development teams need these areas of expertise. Circle the line which represents your assessment of your team's combined skills in these areas (from low on the left to high on the right). Areas of weakness can be overcome by additional staff training or contracting for the services of outside professionals.

Multimedia System Decision Model

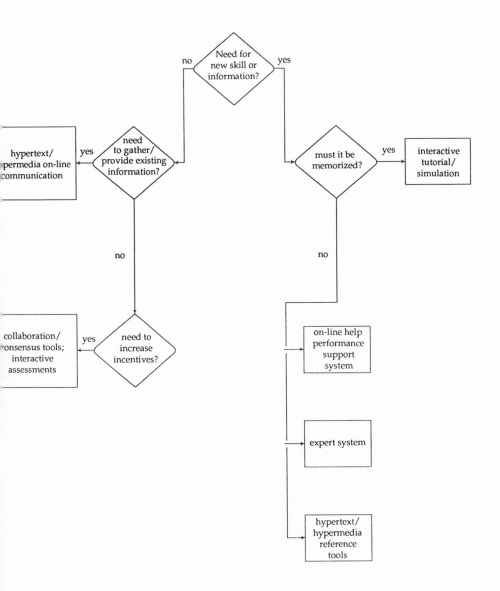

Typical Multimedia Development and Delivery System* (IBM PC Compatible) 1992 costs

Hardware

80386/33 IBM-compatible computer.................................... $1,600.
   120 Mg hard drive, 4 MB memory, 2 diskette drives
   MS DOS 5.0, Microsoft Windows with
   Multimedia Extensions
SuperVGA monitor... 400.
Self-powered speakers... 100.

Motion video board... 900.
   (digitizes live motion video from disc or tape,
   displays it on VA monitor, captures still-frames
VHS camcorder.. 1,200.

(Continued)

---

* Note: Similar systems can be configured for Macintosh and Amiga platforms. Although this system does not support full-motion video compression, it uses standard and rather inexpensive components to support CBT, IVD, computer-based presentations, on-line communication, ID support tools, desktop publishing, expert systems, and performance support tools.

MPC upgrade.. 900.
(CD-ROM player; audio capture and playback board)

Greyscale desktop scanner... 1,100.
Laser printer w/PostScript upgrade....................................... 1,500.

Videodisc player.. 800.
Computer-controlled VCR... 1800.

Modem/fax card.. 400.

Software

Word processing.. 400.
Grammar/style checker.. 400.
Desktop publishing... 600.

Paint program.. 100.
Charting program.. 500.

Menu-based authoring system... 2,000.
Object-oriented hypermedia authoring................................. 600.
Authoring language.. 300.
Animation program... 600.
Hypertext generator... 600.

Flowcharting tool.. 300.
Instructional design support tool.. 1,500.

On-line communication systems.. 200.

Total.. $18,800.

Authoring Tool Checklist

Name of tool _____ Vendor_____

Price _____ Licensing agreement_____

Type of tool/platform _____
    object oriented _____
    menu-based _____
    authoring language _____
    timeline _____
    slideshow _____
    hypertext _____

Branching
    size limit of file _____
    no. of possible branches per response _____

Response types
    multiple choice _____
    true/false _____
    fill in _____
    numeric range _____
    handles misspellings _____
    click on object_____

Ease of use
    length of time to learn basics _____
    length of time to learn advanced techniques _____
    on-line help/tutorials _____
    sample programs/templates _____
    training courses/consultation _____
    novice/expert options _____
    help line/bulletin board _____
    ease of updating _____

Devices supported _____
Graphics/animation supported _____

Record-keeping
    score responses _____
    response time recorded _____
    actual response recorded _____
    leave "bookmark" for re-entry _____
    record repeated attempts _____
    summarize group responses _____

License terms (run-time costs, publishing rights, etc.) _____
_____
_____

Organizations and Publications Related to Multimedia

Association for the Development of Computer-Based Instructional Systems (ADCIS)
1601 West Fifth Avenue
Suite 111
Columbus, OH 43212
(members are primarily professors and developers of computer-based instruction; holds annual meeting; publishes quarterly *Journal of Computer-Based Instruction*.)

Association for Educational Communications & Technology (AECT)
1025 Vermont Ave., N.W.
Washington, D.C. 20005
(members are primarily school/college media specialists; professors of educational technology; some instructional designers in industry; gives awards for student media productions; publishes monthly *Tech Trends* and quarterly research journal, *Educational Technology Research and Development*)

Educational Technology Publications, Inc.
700 Palisade Avenue
Englewood Cliffs, NJ 07632
(publisher of monthly *Educational Technology*, texts and
professional references, and bibliographies on new
technologies)

Future Systems, Inc.
PO Box 26
Falls Church, VA 22040
(publisher of monthly *Multimedia and Videodisc Monitor* as well
as special industry reports and books)

International Interactive Communications Society (IICS)
PO Box 1862
Lake Oswego, OR 97035
(members are producers of multimedia software and hardware;
holds annual conference)

International Television Association (ITVA)
6311 N. O'Connor Rd., LB-51
Irving, TX 75039
(members are corporate/educational video and interactive
video producers; active regional chapters; has a SIG for
interactive video; publishes monthly newsletter)

Meckler Corporation
11 Ferry Lane West
Westport, CT 06880
(publisher of quarterly *Multimedia Review* and related books,
and sponsor of annual conferences on multimedia)

Society for Applied Learning Technology (SALT)
50 Culpeper Street
Warrentown, VA 22186
(members are business, military, and educational producers of interactive media; holds semi-annual conferences/trade shows; publishes monthly *Instruction Delivery Systems* and quarterly research journal, *Journal of Interactive Instruction Development*)

Weingarten Publications, Inc.
38 Chauncey Street
Boston, MA 02111
(publisher of monthly *CBT Directions*, and sponsor of annual conferences on CBT and performance support tools)

Bibliography of
Multimedia Resources

Alessi, S. M., and Trollip, S. R. *Computer-Based Instruction: Methods & Development* (2nd Ed). Englewood Cliffs, NJ: Prentice-Hall, 1990.

Ambron, S., and Hooper, K. *Interactive Multimedia*. Redmond, WA: Microsoft Press, 1988.

Arwady, J., and Gayeski, D. *Using Video: Interactive and Linear Designs*. Englewood Cliffs, NJ: Educational Technology Publications, 1989.

Bergman, R., and Moore, T. *Managing Interactive Video/ Multimedia Projects*. Englewood Cliffs, NJ: Educational Technology Publications, 1990.

Blattner, M. M., and Dannenberg, R. B. *Interactive Multimedia Computing*. Reading, MA: Addison-Wesley, 1992.

Bunzel, M. J. *Multimedia Applications Development*. New York: McGraw-Hill, 1991.

Cabeceiras, J. *The Multimedia Library: Materials Selection & Use*. Orlando, FL: Academic Press, 1991.

Chen, C.-C. *HyperSource on Multimedia-HyperMedia Technologies.* Chicago: American Library Association, 1989.

Gayeski, D. *Interactive Toolkit.* Ithaca, NY: OmniCom Associates, 1987.

Gery, G. J. *Making CBT Happen: Prescriptions for Successful Implementation of Computer-Based Training in Your Organization.* Boston: Weingarten Publications, 1990.

Gery, G. J. *Electronic Performance Support Systems: How & Why to Remake the Workplace Through the Strategic Application of Technology.* Boston: Weingarten Publications, 1991.

Hannafin, M., and Peck, K. *The Design, Development, and Evaluation of Instructional Software.* New York: Macmillan, 1988.

Hodges, M. E. (Ed.) *Multimedia Computing at MIT's Project Athena.* Reading, MA: Addison-Wesley, 1992.

Imke, S. *Interactive Video Management and Production.* Englewood Cliffs, NJ: Educational Technology Publications, 1991.

Iuppa, N. V. *The Multimedia Adventure.* White Plains, NY: Knowledge Industry Publications, 1992.

Kasten, A. S., Miller, R. L., Reeve, V. L., and Sayers, J. H. *Multimedia & Related Technologies: A Glossary of Terms.* Falls Church, VA: Future Systems, 1991.

Lamb, A. *Emerging Technologies & Instruction: Hypertext, Hypermedia, & Interactive Multimedia* (Educational Technology Selected Bibliography Series, Vol. 4). Englewood Cliffs, NJ: Educational Technology Publications, 1991.

Luther, A. C. *Digital Video in the PC Environment.* New York: McGraw-Hill, 1990.

Maddux, C., Johnson, D., and Willis, J. *Educational Computing: Learning with Tomorrow's Technologies.* Boston: Allyn and Bacon, 1992.

McLellan, H. *Virtual Reality* (Educational Technology Selected Bibliography Series, Vol. 6). Englewood Cliffs, NJ: Educational Technology Publications, 1992.

Nix, D., and Spiro, R. (Eds.). *Cognition, Education, & Multimedia: Exploring Ideas in High Technology.* Hillsdale, NJ: Lawrence Erlbaum Associates, 1990.

Schwier, R. *Interactive Video.* Englewood Cliffs, NJ: Educational Technology Publications, 1987.

Schwier, R., and Misanchuk, E. *Interactive Multimedia Instruction.* Englewood Cliffs, NJ: Educational Technology Publications, 1993 (in press).

Waterworth, J. A. *Multimedia: Technology & Applications.* Englewood Cliffs, NJ: Prentice-Hall, 1991.

Weihs, J. *The Integrated Library: Encouraging Access to Multimedia Materials.* Phoenix, AZ: Oryx Press, 1991.

Wilson, S. *Multimedia Design with HyperCard.* Englewood Cliffs, NJ: Prentice-Hall, 1991.

Index